CW00507130

RISEN
indeed

AUTUMN
HOUSE

Copyright ©1992 Revd W. L. White
First published 1993

ISBN 1-873796-16-1

Printed and published by
The Stanborough Press Ltd for
Autumn House Publications
Alma Park, Grantham, NG31 9SL, England

about the author . . .

Revd W. L. (Bill) White was the owner and managing director of a company until, at the age of 40, he felt a call to the Anglican ministry.

Revd White trained at a theological seminary with an evangelical tradition whose principal was Dr. Donald Coggan, later to be Archbishop of Canterbury. Bill White has always been associated with the evangelical wing of the Church of England. For many years he was a close friend and near neighbour of Dr. J. B. Phillips.

Revd Bill White will be remembered by hundreds of thousands of Christians, more especially in the United States, for his long association with the Garden Tomb, Jerusalem. This association lasted for half a century. For much of that time Revd White was Chaplain of the Garden Tomb and Chairman of the Garden Tomb Association. *A Special Place*, published in 1990, is his account of the story of the Garden Tomb.

Many of the insights in this book were first contained in Revd White's famous sermons preached in Jerusalem in front of Christianity's greatest artefact outside of Scripture, the Empty Tomb. *THE PUBLISHERS*

from the author . . .

To the writing of books 'there is no end'. Ecclesiastes 12:12. Tomes and tracts about Jesus Christ are inexhaustible. G. K. Chesterton once titled a book *The Everlasting Man*. Once we acknowledge the uniqueness of Jesus we should not be surprised that, for multitudes of men and women, history is His-story, and that *His* life is the foundation of *our* lives.

He never wrote a book — yet all the world's great libraries could not contain the books written about Him.

He never composed a song — yet the world's music publishers together could not match the songs He has inspired.

He never founded a college — yet the world's universities cannot boast as many students as He enrols.

He never marshalled an army — yet no general ever gained more volunteers, nor won more captives.

It can be argued fairly that the fulfilment of God's redemptive purpose for mankind was compressed into eight weeks of human madness and divine miracle.

This book tells the story of those eight weeks. Dorothy L. Sayers has called the events they contained 'the greatest drama ever staged'. These events are timeless in their application.   *REVD W. L. WHITE, Corfe Castle*

abbreviations

JBP J. B. Phillips, *The New Testament in Modern English* (1972) Harper Collins.
LB The Living Bible (1971) Tyndale House.
NAS New American Standard, A. J. Holman Company.
NEB New English Bible (1970) Oxford and Cambridge.
NIV New International Version (1979) Hodder and Stoughton.
RAV Revised Authorized Version (1982) Samuel Bagster.
REB Revised English Bible (1989) Oxford and Cambridge.
RSV Revised Standard Version (1952) Oxford.
   Where no version is specified the quotation has been taken from the King James Version.
   All Bible quotations are rendered in italics.

RISEN
indeed

contents

1 JERUSALEM IN TURMOIL

'When he entered Jerusalem the whole city went wild with excitement. "Who is this?" people asked.' (Matthew 21:10, NEB.)

Palm Sunday. The carpenter of Nazareth was arriving in the holy city to make His final appeal.

The arrival of Jesus brought crisis to the Jewish religious establishment. To the priesthood Jesus was a cult leader who threatened the *status quo* and, hence, must be eliminated. Further to that, the arrival of Jesus brought confusion to the minds of the people. Most of them had no personal link with the Man from Galilee. Only a few would have had first-hand experience of His miracles. Amid the turmoil there were group tensions.

● **The loud shouters;** *'They cried Hosanna!'*

The word Hosanna means 'save us we pray'. The trouble is that many who will chant hosanna in public are not always anxious for salvation to affect their private lives. They may have a lot to say in church circles, but they are short of breath when it's time to give a testimony in the canteen or board room.

Jesus never played down the demands of discipleship. Sooner or later we have to decide between allegiance to Christ or compromise with the world.

● **The palm wavers;** *'They took branches and strewed them in the way.'*

This section of the crowd was in the procession because they were attracted to anything that promised to be sensational. They were people of good will; not hostile to Jesus. Willing to join a demonstration, they were, as a rule, only available for special occasions!

Today campaigns, conferences and conventions can fill

arenas but, in many cases, the 'palm waving' fails to muster the foot-slogging of ongoing commitment. A dictionary is the only place where Success comes before Work!

We hear much about the failure of the clergy. Most of them will acknowledge their spiritual frailty. Part of the problem is that whenever the Lord needs to call a man to become a pastor he has only the laity to choose from!

There may be a gap between pulpit and pew. Too often there is a *gulf* between pew and pavement. A few days after that procession of palms, it was on that very same road that Jesus paused to weep over Jerusalem. He cared about humanity; hence His disciples must share His social concern. If nominal churchmen are content to choose golf and gardening to the exclusion of charity concerns and community service, then they shouldn't complain if public life becomes dominated by agnostic agitators.

Did the Palm Sunday crowd merely change its tune on Good Friday? There is no gospel evidence to suggest that those who shouted 'Hosanna' on Sunday chanted 'Crucify' on Friday. Amid growing tension did they simply keep quiet?

It is one thing to sit in a cosy clique and deplore the media output of secular morality and liberal theology. But when did *you* last protest by letter or phone as a positive expression of Christian conscience? Too many Christians are slow to stand up and be counted.

● **The self-seekers;** *It was reported that Jesus had raised Lazarus from the dead. . . . 'For this cause the people also met him, for that they heard that he had done this miracle.'* (John 12:18.)

One section of the crowd was present because it was rumoured that there was a new movement worth following. Christ's mission to redeem the world was not the magnet that drew them out. Their enthusiasm was that He might produce a political 'quick-fix'.

There are two grades of Christian discipleship. First, those who are pleased to *use* the Church in any way it can *serve* them; second, those who seek to *serve* the Lord in any way He can *use* them.

A man dreamt there were shops in heaven. In his dream he entered one and asked for the fruit of the Spirit. An angelic assistant informed him, 'We don't sell fruit, we only supply seed.'

No fruit without root!

There's another figure in the Palm Sunday procession we must not forget.

● **The donkey.**

Does this seem flippant?

The ass has become a symbol of stupidity.

Sad to say, much of the world's sorrow has been brought about by man's stupidity. He was given authority over the animal creation, yet nothing in nature is more asinine than the behaviour of some humans! Jesus was ashamed of the petty jealousies and selfish squabbles He found among God's people. *'What can I say that the men of this generation are like — what sort of men are they? They are like children sitting in the market-place and calling out to each other, "We played at weddings for you, but you wouldn't dance, and we played at funerals for you, and you wouldn't cry!"'* (Luke 7:32, JBP.)

Before we get too despondent about asinine antics, remember there's a positive quality associated with the donkey. Among all the animals, man has not found a more faithful burden-bearer than the ass. It was most likely a donkey that carried Mary to Bethlehem. Another one was on hand for Palm Sunday. He waved no palm and shouted no hosanna, yet he was closer to the Lord than most of the others. His was not an easy task. Sweaty clothes on his back, branches under his feet, and the noise of a shouting multitude.

Inexperienced as the animal was, he carried the Master and responded to the touch of His hand.

Isn't that discipleship?

The routine of daily life is about as far as most of us can see of the road ahead. It is amid the hum-drum that God calls us even if, like the donkey, we seem to be 'tethered to a post'. Perhaps, when He thinks we are ready, the Master will ask us to carry Him on a more inspiring journey. At first, however, discipleship may mean being tied to a position that is not of our choosing.

2 ANGER IN THE SANCTUARY

The accounts of Jesus 'cleansing the temple' follow those of His triumphal entry into Jerusalem.

The temple area covered thirty acres. The ground that surrounded the main sanctuary and holy place was divided into various courts. The largest court, which was located on the south side of the enclosure, was the Court of the Gentiles. Next, inside the Wall of Partition, were the Courts of the Women, of the Israelites, and of the Priests. There were also small ante-rooms.

That is the setting.

The *question* is: '*Why was Jesus so angry?*'

It all happened during Passover Week. Passover was the major religious festival of Judaism. The Law decreed that every adult male Jew who lived within twenty miles of Jerusalem was bound to attend.

Passover, however, attracted Jews from well beyond this radius. Indeed, it was not only Palestinian Jews who observed the feasts. Although Jews had become scattered throughout the known world, they never forgot their faith or their ancestral homeland. It was the dream and aim of every Jew to celebrate at least one Passover in Jerusalem.

No need to ask why Jerusalem was so crowded at that season of the year.

At Passover time a Temple Tax was levied on every adult male Jew. The half shekel he was required to contribute was equal to two days' pay for a working man. For commercial purposes many currencies were used in Palestine. Silver coins of Rome, Greece, Egypt and other regions were all in circulation. However, this Temple Tax had to be paid only in shekelim or a special coinage of the Hebrew sanctuary. Other currencies were foreign and, therefore, 'unclean'!

The pilgrims who arrived for Passover brought with them a wide variety of currencies. So, inside the temple courts sat the 'money changers'. They provided a necessary service. But all manner of irregularities surrounded their activities by the time of Jesus. Rates of exchange were manipulated. The business had become a 'rip-off'.

Besides the money changers, the temple precincts were filled with merchants selling oxen, sheep and doves. Many pilgrims wished to make a thank offering to God. Most events in life were commemorated by an appropriate sacrifice. Again, it appeared a helpful service that the tokens for the purchase of sacrificial animals should be on sale near the place of sacrifice. Alas, a monopoly situation had developed. The Law decreed that the animals sacrificed should be 'without blemish'. To enforce this rule the temple authorities appointed inspectors who provided a 'seal of approval' — subject, of course, to an extra fee! Should a worshipper bring his own offering or, perhaps, buy one outside the temple precincts, it was unlikely that the inspector would give it his official approval. The worshipper would be involved in acquiring a replacement purchase.

Monopolies affect price levels. A pair of doves bought for the equivalent of 10 pence outside the temple cost 50 pence inside! Religion had become a racket.

We begin to see why Jesus was angry. . . .

In addition to the cartel run by the wheeler-dealers, there was another important consideration: God's house was being desecrated. Temple worship was interrupted by irreverence. Reverence is an instinctive response of the human to the divine. Worship without reverence can be blasphemy. In this matter the church is no less vulnerable than the temple. . . .

Two contrasting attitudes can endanger authentic Christian worship. They are: *ritualism* and *'rutualism'*. On the one hand, there is the fussiness that puts ceremonial detail before spiritual inspiration. On the other hand, there is a drabness that allows dull routine to stifle spiritual imagination — *rut*-ualism.

Worship can become so formalized that profound words

of Scripture and prayer are recited like a page from an auctioneer's catalogue. This happens when worship is not linked to a recognition of God's majesty and holiness.

In the temple court of Jerusalem there was bickering about coins, argument about costs, and a clatter and a chatter that turned the Gate of the Sanctuary into a noisy street market.

The righteous wrath of Jesus arose because God's law was being misinterpreted. The routine and paraphernalia of animal sacrifice was, in itself, irrelevant. For centuries the Hebrew prophets had warned about this; *'Listen to the Lord. Hear what he is telling you! I am sick of your sacrifices. Don't bring me any more of them. I don't want your fat rams; I don't want to see the blood from your offerings. Who wants sacrifices when you have no sorrow for your sins? The incense you bring me is a stench in my nostrils. Your holy celebrations of new moon and the Sabbath, and your special days for fasting — even your most pious meetings — are all frauds!'* (Isaiah 1:10-13, LB.)

The anger of Jesus was tinged with disappointment and sorrow. At the deepest level Jesus was angry because God's people had become unholy and self-righteous. In Mark's gospel there are three words which do not appear in other accounts: *'Doesn't the Scripture say, "My house shall be called a house of prayer for all nations"? But you have turned it into a thieves' kitchen!'* (Mark 11:17, JBP.)

The Court of the Gentiles was the largest of the courts within the confines of Temple Mount. And it was this very area that had been requisitioned by the Jerusalem Ministry of Farming and Trade! The Court of the Gentiles was the only part of the temple area where a non-Jew could enter. It was to this spot that a God-fearing Gentile might come to meditate, pray and learn something of God's law and love revealed in Scripture. Yet this was the very place where the bargaining and bedlam had rendered meditation impossible.

When Jesus *'had made a whip of cords, he drove them all out of the temple, with the sheep and the oxen'.* (John 2:15, RAV.) Does Christ's action provide a justification for violence? The narrative itself answers the question. If Jesus was acting as a law-breaker, the temple authorities would have been most willing to arrest Him. Remember the temple was outside Roman jurisdiction, so there was no case of *civil* disobedience. The temple was guarded by a Jewish militia. No Roman soldier could set foot in the temple.

When the disciples witnessed what happened, Christ's anger reminded them of a Scripture; *'The zeal of thy house has eaten me up.'* The righteous anger of Jesus was not theatrical petulance. In terms of physical force He could have been instantly outnumbered and overpowered. The fact that He was *not* restrained by temple 'police' reveals that His moral authority vindicated His exposure of the priestly authorities who turned a blind eye to the violation of this holy place.

One Old Testament passage offers a stirring commentary and provides prophetic significance to Christ's messianic action; *'The Lord, whom you seek, will suddenly come to his temple, even the Messenger of the covenant . . . . But who can endure the day of his coming? And who shall stand when he appears? For he is like a refiner's fire. . . . He will purify the sons of Levi, and purge them as gold and silver, that they may offer to the Lord an offering in righteousness.'* (Malachi 3:1-4, RAV.)

Few people can combine great indignation with quiet dignity. Jesus was not inciting a 'rough-house'. Armed with the authority of God's law, He was evicting trespassers.

3 THE PERILS OF PRIESTHOOD

You have heard of the 'Seven Deadly Sins'. How about the 'Seven Serious Sins of Religion'? They are listed in Matthew 23:13-36. Churchgoers who still sing about 'Gentle Jesus meek and mild' should read these verses intently!

Jesus registered words of devastating denunciation — and targeted them at the religious leaders of His day.

The 'Seven Woes' against the Scribes and Pharisees have been described as 'the rolling thunder' of Christ's wrath. They are like thunder in their unanswerable severity and like lightning in their unsparing exposure. They illuminate as they strike!

In these 'Woes' Jesus repeatedly describes the Scribes and the Pharisees as hypocrites. The Greek word *hupokrites* came to be associated with stage drama and is the regular Greek word for an actor. It referred to one who wore a theatrical costume that might depict a regal role in a play but whose real life was very different. Jesus saw these men as participants in a game of religious charades.

The 'Seven Serious Sins of Religion' should be re-examined in terms of today.

● ' "Woe to you, teachers of the law and Pharisees, you hypocrites! You shut the kingdom of heaven in men's faces." ' (Matthew 23:13, NIV.)

In our age the equivalent danger might be when we confuse the seeker. There is spiritual need in every life. We need to beware lest we allow the 'Way-in' to God's kingdom to become obstructed by ecclesiastical turnstiles or cheapened by spurious duty-free passes! Jesus seems to warn of a double danger in that the door could be locked as well as closed. ' "You have taken away the key to knowledge

. . . and hindered those who were entering." ' (Luke 11:52, NIV.) The apostles taught that Scripture is a key to understanding salvation through Christ. How disturbing when late twentieth-century teachers of theology handle the Bible in a manner that fails to unlock the truths of the Gospel and causes some to assume the 'Faith' to be founded on myths.

A vicar, visiting a sick parishioner, suggested a Bible reading. When he took the bedside Bible he found a large proportion of the pages missing. The patient explained; 'I have listened to your sermons for ten years, and I remove from my Bible everything you suggest is unscientific, uncertain or unreliable.'

In facing Christ's denunciation of the Pharisees, it must not be assumed that He condemned every aspect of their teaching. After all, they enunciated the great principles of the ten commandments which rightly demanded reverence and respect. Their beliefs went off-centre when an infinity of man-made rules and regulations were added to make religious observance a bewildering maze of legalistic imposition.

A simple test can be applied to every religious source. Does it give a person 'wings' to lift them up, or add weights to hold them down?

● ' *"Woe to you, teachers of the Law and Pharisees, you hypocrites! You devour widows' houses and for a show make lengthy prayers."* ' (Matthew 23:14, NIV.)

According to Jewish tradition, a rabbi could not be paid for his teaching ministry. All rabbis were required to follow a trade so that they could support themselves. On the other hand, in Jesus' day, it had become widely publicized that to support a rabbi was a commitment of special piety. Jesus knew that some impressionable women often fell victim to unscrupulous and self-seeking rabbis. Financially such men did devour widows' houses. It remains a sad fact that women continue to be imposed upon by religious charlatans. Our equivalent danger is that we may overload the susceptible.

The long prayers of the Pharisees were notorious. They were offered in public places and in such profusion that the pietism was performance-perfect. Even sincere intercession can become undisciplined. Public prayers that 'hit the roof' do not always reach heaven.

• ' *"Woe unto you, teachers of the law and Pharisees, you hypocrites! You travel over land and sea to win a single convert, and when he becomes one, you make him twice as much a son of hell as you are."* ' (Matthew 23:15, NIV.)

In the ancient world Jews were often hated. Their separatism and contempt for gentile nations caused hostility.

Yet, there was a compelling attraction in Judaism. The idea of one God was a wonderful thing in a world confused by a multitude of deities. The ethical purity and high moral standards of Judaism challenged nations steeped in immorality.

Yes, gentiles were attracted to the God of Israel.

First, there were 'God-fearers'; people who accepted the teaching of the Hebrew Law and Prophets but took no part in ceremonial observances.

Second, there were proselytes; it was the aim of Pharisees to turn a God-fearer into a proselyte — a full convert who would submit to ceremonial law and circumcision and, therefore, become in the fullest sense a Jew.

The sin of the Pharisees was that they sought to lead others to Pharisaism rather than to God. A proselyte could become more hidebound in the dogmas of tradition than subservient to the truths that at first attracted him.

Our equivalent danger is that we might link others to a sect rather than the Saviour. In an era of deepening despondency and disillusionment, the jargon of New Age cults offer a persuasive package of 'Eastern promise' that breeds egocentricity.

If Satan cannot torpedo the Ark of Christ's Church, he seeks to get passengers and crew all pushing to one side of the ship so that the vessel will list or capsize!

- ' "*Woe to you, teachers of the law and Pharisees, you hypocrites! You give a tenth of your spices — mint, dill and cummin. But you have neglected the more important matters of the law — justice, mercy and faithfulness. You should have practised the latter, without neglecting the former.*" ' (Matthew 23:23, NIV.)

Tithing was an essential part of the Jewish economy. One tenth of the produce of their land was given to God. Fastidious Pharisees did not stop at that; they tithed their garden herbs like mint, rue and cummin. They were meticulous in the minor details, but were sidestepping deeper and more fundamental issues of life and faith.

In *any* church environment there is an equivalent danger. Namely, that we exaggerate the unimportant.

The most vivid illustration given by Jesus of this danger is when He called the Pharisees 'blind guides' who would 'strain out a gnat and swallow a camel'.

In Jewish eyes both an insect and a camel were 'unclean'. The Pharisee would strain his wine through muslin gauze to avoid any possible impurity but, said Jesus, he will go on to swallow a camel! The humorous picture must have raised a laugh. But it remains the perfect picture of a person who has completely lost his sense of proportion.

- ' "*Woe to you, teachers of the law and Pharisees, you hypocrites! You clean the outside of the cup and dish, but inside they are full of greed and self-indulgence.*" ' (Matthew 23:25, NIV.)

This 'woe' is an extension of the previous one since it exposes a contrast between belief and behaviour. Uncleanness was a recurring theme in Jewish law. However, this factor was a matter of ceremonial, not hygiene. The Jew was unclean if he touched a dead body or came into contact with a gentile. The whole matter became so adsurdly complicated and lost all spiritual meaning.

Jesus was pointing out that food and drink inside the cleansed vessel might have been obtained by extortion or theft; that the *content* of the cup was the source of intemperance.

In our decade the equivalent danger would be that we dodge the fundamentals. . . .

These days commercials for washing powders and liquids that combat stains and smells are flashed before our eyes every few minutes of the day! Then, following the TV 'break', the programme takes up again. . . . As it does so, we note that the language is not as 'sanitized' as the commercials want our homes to be. The soap opera plots that merge with the perfume ads are as socially unwholesome as the dirt that detergents claim to banish. Apparently our concern is with hygiene only in matters external. . . .

Let's not be 'custard Christians', upset over trifles. Stand firm for principles. But how many congregations have been split down the middle over the colour of a new carpet, the introduction of a new hymn-book or a change in the time of a service? Jesus said, *'My peace I leave with you.'* The solemn fact is that too often arguments over matters of small importance disturb that peace. . . .

● ' "Woe to you, teachers of the law and Pharisees, you hypocrites! You are like whitewashed tombs, which look beautiful on the outside but on the inside are full of dead men's bones and everything unclean." ' (Matthew 23:27, NIV.)

Every Jew understood this scene. A common place for a tomb was by a wayside. Anyone who touched a corpse was defiled. Anyone who came in contact with a tomb was unclean.

In the springtime of the year, roads in Palestine were crowded with pilgrims. Thousands of Jews would travel to Jerusalem to celebrate Passover. Imagine what a disaster it would be for a man who had travelled many days to tread on a tomb by accident and, therefore, be barred from the festival! Because of such a possibility, it became a practice, immediately before Passover, to whitewash wayside tombs so that no pilgrim should be caught unawares and rendered 'unclean'.

As men travelled to the Holy City, tombs would glint white, standing out like bright beacons, but actually containing dead men's bones and corruption.

There are those who stand on the perimeter of spiritual things. Timid souls who would like to believe, but somehow feel that religion is not for them. For such people, a first encounter with Christians will be crucial. . . .

The general public demands a high standard of professing Christians. Their assessment is sometimes unfair. They will contrast the best 'pagan' they know, with the worst churchgoer of their acquaintance. They are on the lookout for false piety and spiritual snobbery. They can spot them at a hundred paces.

When 'secular man' comes in contact with Christian worship we must ensure that he finds it meaningful and relevant. Even the casual 'pew-squatter' can sense when liturgy is ostentation and when 'rite' is wrong.

Bible-based preaching is a fundamental need for any congregation. 'Religious novelties' will never woo a nation back to God.

● ' "Woe to you, teachers of the law and Pharisees, you hypocrites! You build tombs for the prophets and decorate the graves of the righteous. And you say, 'If we had lived in the days of our forefathers, we would not have taken part with them in shedding the blood of the prophets.' So you testify against yourselves that you are the descendants of those who murdered the prophets. . . . from the blood of righteous Abel to the blood of Zechariah son of Berakiah, whom you murdered between the temple and the altar." ' (Matthew 23:29-31, 35, NIV.)

The charge of Jesus: that in Israel's history righteous

men from Abel to Zechariah had been murdered.

Why mention these two?

The former is well known; the latter is known only from a grim little account in an obscure passage, 2 Chronicles 24:21.

In the Hebrew Bible, Genesis is the first book; but, unlike our order, 2 Chronicles is the last. Hence it might be said that Abel's is the first murder in the Old Testament, and that of Zechariah the last. From beginning to end, the history of Israel was the rejection of God's messengers.

Jesus criticized the Pharisees for their concern for memorials to conveniently remote events. They professed to reverence the memory of the prophets killed by their forefathers. The suggestion of Jesus is that if the prophets were still alive those Pharisees would have repeated the crime. (Matthew 23:31.)

During the Christian era reformers and martyrs have lived — and died — for our Gospel faith. We need to remember them.

More importantly, we need to remember their Gospel: salvation by grace through faith in Jesus Christ alone. Remember it and, through repentance and self-surrender, accept the gifts that God gives us through His grace: faith and, what comes with it, the assurance of salvation.

At all costs let us resist the modern Pharisees who urge us to work for salvation through performance. Salvation is not through performance, but promise.

'For it is by grace you have been saved, through faith — and this not from yourselves, it is the gift of God — not of works, so that no one can boast.' (Ephesians 2:8, 9, NIV.)

4 GETHSEMANE

Calvary was the outcome of a *preceding* crisis, a decisive conflict faced and fought in Gethsemane.

There has been much debate as to where the main responsibility for the crucifixion should be laid. Were the Jews to blame? Could Rome have intervened? Was Pilate a 'pawn' in the game? Was Judas worse than Caiaphas? These questions are purely academic since, in fact, events were arguably dictated by Jesus Himself.

Script writers and commentators speak of 'the tragedy of the cross'. That is wrong. The cross was not a tragedy but a triumph. Jesus was not a martyr. In the end a martyr has no choice. But listen to Jesus: ' "*I lay down my life that I may take it again. No one takes it from me; . . . I have power to lay it down, and I have power to take it again.*" ' (John 10:17, 18, RAV.)

What a claim! Unique! In the light of that claim, if you want to understand the victory of Calvary, you begin at Gethsemane.

It was in the Garden of Gethsemane that Jesus agonized; '*Father, if it be possible, let this cup pass . . . .*' (Matthew 26:39.)

The anticipation of suffering can be harder to bear than the actual physical pain. The crisis Jesus faced in Gethsemane, however, was far deeper than any recognized level of human anguish. (Hebrews 5:7.) It is inadequate to examine the crisis of Gethsemane without relating it to other events in the Holy Week drama.

- **Preparation for the Last Supper.** (Mark 14:13-15.)

Some have asked why the location for the last supper was not divulged to all the apostles. The answer lies in the fact that Jesus was aware of a betrayal being plotted by Judas. Judas had to seek a moment when crowds were absent. Any attempt to apprehend Jesus in the temple precincts would have caused a riot. Had Judas overheard where the supper was to be, a contingent from the Sanhedrin would have made their arrest at the house of the upper room. Judas did not know the venue until he arrived with the other disciples. He left the upper room on his own on the pretext of 'shopping' for the Passover Feast. (John 13:27-30.)

Jesus *was* in control.

Had He been arrested in the upper room we should have been denied the vital teaching and the wonderful prayer contained in John's gospel, chapters 14 to 17.

● The legacy of the upper room.

At the last supper Jesus had only a brief span of freedom left. His 'last words' bequeathed a sublime legacy of timeless truth. John chapters 14 to 17 have been a source of devotion for millions of believers through nineteen centuries. The whole atmosphere of these chapters captures the intimate fellowship between the Master and His men.

When Jesus began the parable of the vine (John 15:1-10), the disciples would immediately catch the picture of the Golden Vine that trailed round the four marbled pillars that flanked the entrance to the temple; the vine that was emblematic of the Jewish people. The Lord Himself identified with the vine.

Three key words emerge from Christ's parable of the vine and the branches:

Being . . . *'I am the vine, you are the branches.'*

It is only as we recognize who He is, that we can accept ourselves and come to terms with life's circumstances. God is never in a hurry! Blossoms that have been 'forced' soon wilt, and some Christians appear to display a 'greenhouse effect'. Beware of 'hothouse theology' that offers instant holiness without tilling and hoeing.

Growing . . . *'Without me you can do nothing.'*

Life never stands still, and development is a demand of

nature. Sun, soil and rain are elements of growth. In the quest for Christian character there will be no triumph without testing. If our hand muscles were never tensed, we should never get a grip on anything. *'Every branch is pruned that it may yield more fruit.'*

Resting . . . ' *"A good tree does not bear bad fruit."* ' (Luke 6:43, RAV.)

No farmer ever passed a sleepless night worrying that his plum tree might produce crab apples. When lives are open to the seed of God's word, the fruit of the Spirit will appear in due season.

Someone coined the phrase 'religious *hectivity*'. The phrase implies a tense emotionalism that rushes from campaign to convention and on to the next campaign until Spring Harvest becomes an autumn gale! Sanctification is not a matter of wrestling but of resting.

If there was ever a moment in history when *everything* was at stake, and a situation of *eternal* significance existed, it was in the upper room on the night of Christ's betrayal.

Focus on the tension surrounding the last supper. Think of the miracle of Christ's quiet serenity. Ponder the unhurried poise and divine authority that challenged fears and frets. While the disciples were bickering over status, the Master washed their feet in an object lesson in leadership. When they plied Him with questions He gave them an answer that quells every human quandary: *'I am the way, the truth, and the life.'* (John 14:6.)

Jesus was answering a question by Thomas who voiced the perplexity of all the apostles: *'Lord we don't know where you are going, so how can we know the way?'* In a deeper sense he articulated the question that lurks in the heart of everyone. Anthropologists affirm that in every tribe two factors are evident: an instinct to reverence something beyond oneself, and an in-built response to a code of moral behaviour.

Every soul has a capacity for God.

In some sense, a primitive tribesman may be better off than a cynical scientist.

Modern man has a 'God-shaped' blank in his mind. And the rising tide of violence in our 'progressive' society springs from a rejection of the one true God and an ignorance of His commandments.

Christ's answer to Thomas's question is the most profound remedy for human disease:

'I am the way' — Without Him there is no GOING.

'I am the truth' — Without Him there is no KNOWING.

'I am the life' — Without Him there is no GROWING.

His Way can satisfy the will; His Truth can satisfy the mind; His Life can satisfy the soul.

'I am the way'; His Word leads to SAFETY.

In all His parables Jesus made it plain that the opposite of being in 'the Way' is to be lost. *'The Son of Man has come to seek and to save that which is lost.'*

We don't get lost intentionally. When Jesus answered Thomas he established a dual truth. Jesus Christ is the ONLY way.

' *"No man comes to the Father except through me."* ' (John 14:6, NIV.) This phrase raises a flood of queries. Many alternative routes to salvation are on offer. There is the way of humanism via Mother Nature and Brother Guru. There is the way of materialism via evolution and education. There is the way of ecclesiasticism via rites and ritual. The New Testament declares: *'There is one God, and one mediator between God and men, the man Christ Jesus.'* (1 Timothy 2:5.)

Any suggested path to God that does not put Jesus Christ in the centre will prove a cul-de-sac.

Another aspect of this truth is that Christ is the OPEN WAY. When people sought Him, Jesus did not present an obstacle course but said, 'I am the door.'

'I am the truth . . . ' — His word leads to CERTAINTY.

Old Testament prophets spoke about 'the truth'. But no

man had ever embodied the Truth. In academic affairs the character of the individual may not greatly alter his effectiveness as a lecturer. But when a person proposes to teach moral truth, character will make a profound difference. Paul spoke of the *'truth as it is in Jesus'*. (Ephesians 4:21, REB.) Understood like this, truth will make tremendous demands upon our Christian life and thinking.

When Paul visited the centre of Greek culture *circa* AD 51 *'the Athenians and the foreigners who lived there spent their time doing nothing but talking about and listening to the latest ideas'.* (Acts 17:21, NIV.) Who said 'times change'? Education without revelation only produces clever religious theories. . . . A bishop once said that in his diocese he had several clergy with double-first degrees — but he could not put one of them in charge of a whelk stall! The words 'wisdom' and 'knowledge' cannot be used interchangeably. The most knowledgeable can be the least wise.

• Truth demands intellectual clarity.

We are wrong if we imagine that a majority of people have no interest in 'the truth'. Many 'fancy religions' have emerged over the years. Some eccentric sects have come into being because mainstream Christianity made the love of God too narrow or failed to proclaim the Gospel clearly.

Truth is the fruit of insight. Jesus rarely argued. Apart from insight, truth is sometimes the reward of searching. A dedicated scientist is prepared to set aside a favourite theory if the discovery of a new truth reveals it to be unsafe.

One great failing of Christian congregations is that they tend to repeat ancient dogmas to people outside of the Church when they have not thought through the doctrines for themselves. If there are too many empty pews, perhaps it is because too many occupied pulpits fail to proclaim the Christian Gospel simply and clearly.

• Truth demands intellectual humility.

The bedrock of belief is 2 Timothy 3:16, 17: *'All scripture is given by inspiration of God and is profitable for doctrine, for reproof, for correction, for instruction in righteousness: that the man of God may be perfect, throughly furnished unto all good works.'*

In decades long gone the English were called 'the people of the Book — and that Book the Bible'. Even today, per capita, there are probably more Bibles in Britain than in any other European country. But the Bible is no longer a controlling influence upon national life.

Many still approve of sending Bibles abroad. But at home the Bible has become a sort of religious 'juke-box' offering family favourites on demand.

'Suffer little children to come . . .' — at the christening.

'The Lord's my Shepherd . . . ' — at the wedding.

'In my Father's house are many mansions . . .' — at the funeral.

We feel superior to people of other lands who have idols of silver and brass in their homes. But a false *mental* image is no less delusive than a false *metal* image! Jesus said He would send *'the Spirit of truth . . . he will guide you'*. (John 16:12-15.)

● **Truth demands intellectual sincerity.**

In New Testament times, when marble pillars were being made, sometimes a flaw would appear. A rogue workman would fill the flaw with wax (*cera*) and polish it over. When subject to the elements, rain would wash out the wax and the fault would be revealed. A perfect marble pillar was said to be *'sine cera'* (without wax). When you sign your next letter 'yours sincerely', you are saying 'I am without wax'!

Human nature being what it is, there are flaws in all of us. We try to cover them up. Jesus, in telling them to beware of the hypocrisy of the Pharisees, said: ' *"Nothing is covered up that will not be revealed, or hidden that will not be known. Whatever you have said in the dark shall*

*be heard in the light, and what you have whispered in private
rooms shall be proclaimed upon the housetop."* ' (Luke 12:2,
3, RSV.)

'I am the LIFE . . . ' — His word leads to FUL-
FILMENT.

When Jesus talked of 'life' it was more than a reference
to mortality. He had already told Martha, *'He who believes
in me, though he die yet shall he live.'* When a Christian
talks of eternity he does not mean a mere extension of ex-
istence, or an absorption into the infinite! The message of
the apostolic church was not some theory of survival but
a vital conviction that faith in the risen Christ spelt abun-
dant life both here and now and there and then.

Universalism is an attitude widely prevalent today. It implies that all religions are just different highways that will
eventually converge at some celestial roundabout. We should
not accept a platform that places the Lord Jesus Christ as
'another prophet' alongside Buddha, Muhammad or Moses.
Jesus Christ is the ultimate revelation of God to man. He
is the Messiah of Israel, the Saviour of the world, and Lord
of the universe. (Colossians 1:15-21.)

Take a close look at His teaching and ministry in the
gospels and you will discover that every facet of His divine
personality was counterbalanced by a complementary attribute. With Christ's wisdom was humour; with His percep-
tion, courage; with His anger, compassion; with His authority,
humility.

He came from the realm of eternity into the arena of
history. He shared our humanity that we might gain the
hope of His immortality. He became Son of Man, that we
might be sons of God. On earth He received no worldly
status. At birth He was laid in a borrowed manger. In death
He was laid in a borrowed tomb.

Great men come and go. *He* is the Great Contemporary.

He has the whole world in His hands, and yet His hands
are tied by a world that ignores Him.

● The timing of the betrayal.

This poses a key question. If Judas left the upper room after sundown to inform the chief priest where Jesus was, *Why was Jesus not arrested until around midnight?*

The gospels do not answer all of our questions. It is clear that some complications developed behind the scenes. About four hours elapsed from the time Judas left the upper room until the moment of his betrayal in Gethsemane.

In Mark 14:51, 52 John Mark, whose mother's house later became the headquarters for the apostolic assembly, was the young man who 'followed afar off' and then lost his pyjamas in a struggle with the militia in the garden.

Whatever reasons may be offered to explain the delay, it is impossible to escape the conclusion that the arrest took place only because Jesus had deliberately waited to be taken!

Instead of the agony in Gethsemane, Jesus could have been over the hill and back in Bethany long before the mob set foot in the garden.

Gethsemane was the focal point of crisis. There Jesus *waited* — one hour and *waited* — two hours and *waited* — three hours.

In the light of this it is easier to grasp the significance of Christ's agony and travail of soul. Suppose there is a bomb under the chair where you now sit. You can hear the clock-fuse ticking away. Could you curb every instinct to run?

Because Jesus waited in Gethsemane, we can know forgiveness of sins and resurrection to life everlasting.

5 PONTIUS PILATE

One of the stranger quirks of history must be that the name of the rather small-fry Roman Governor who administered Judaea between AD 26 and 36 has been echoed by millions of voices every week for sixteen centuries!

The name 'Pontius Pilate' has become engraved in the Christian Creed via the cryptic phrase 'He suffered under Pontius Pilate . . . .'.

A businessman was sitting opposite a clergyman in a restaurant. He noticed an unusual badge in the lapel of the other man's jacket. It was in the shape of a silver question mark. 'May I ask what your badge signifies?'

'Certainly! It represents the most important question ever asked!'

'What might that be?'

'It was put by a Roman governor nearly 2,000 years ago.'

'And what was the question?'

What shall I do . . . with Jesus who is called Christ? (Matthew 27:22, NIV.)

The background of that question warrants attention. On the day the question was first put, you could sum up Pilate's dilemma as 'a drama in four episodes'.

● **The encounter with Christ that was inevitable.** *When they had bound him, they led him away, and delivered him to Pilate.* (Matthew 27:2.)

It may be that Pilate had already realized the meeting was unavoidable. It is most unlikely that the name of Jesus of Nazareth was unknown to him. He would have received reports. The position of the Roman procurator in Jerusalem was a delicate one. The Jews had proved a difficult race to subdue, and even more difficult to rule. Pilate had a Roman MI5 to inform him of sources that might threaten the peace of the region. It is by no means unlikely that the information

Pilate had on Jesus was more detailed than any one of the gospels!

At official functions the name of Jesus would feature in discussion.

It is clear that Pilate's wife had knowledge of Jesus and His teachings.

Perhaps Pilate had filed Jesus as a 'persuasive but harmless prophet'!

Suddenly, however, a new and ugly note appeared. Was there a political slant in His preaching? Hints of a link with the terrorist zealots? Pilate sensed a crisis. He had heard about Jesus, but now . . . it's for real! He had received reports of the person of Jesus. Now he is faced with the reality of the presence of Jesus.

The Roman official was no longer dealing with a security file. Jesus was standing before Pilate and, to his dying day, Pilate would never forget the hours that followed.

● **The evasion of Christ that was impossible.** '*What shall I do?*'

Pilate faced an issue that could not be shelved.

To understand his dilemma we must analyse the situation.

Consider the pressures on Pilate.

There was the demand of the priests and Scribes who wanted Jesus eliminated.

Pilate knew that Jesus had exposed the Jewish leaders. Their pride of position had been challenged, and their religious hypocrisy revealed; ' "*If we let him go on like this, everyone will believe in him, and then the Romans will come and take away both our place and our nation.*" ' (John 11:48, NIV.)

Pressure at top level insisted that Jesus must die.

And there were other pressures on Pilate.

Unexpectedly his wife urged that Jesus should be vindicated. Perhaps a woman's intuition sensed the evil plotting. When people have servants, they get the latest news from the local market! When Pilate's wife rose early after a disturbed night, she sent the message, *'Have nothing to do with this just man.'*

It is plain to see that after Pilate had faced Jesus his conscience was pricked and his mind gave judgement: *'I find no fault in him.'*

In the light of the growing pressures, consider the predicament of the man.

He wanted to do the right thing, but saw what might happen if he followed his convictions. The Pharisees were watching his every move; *'If you let this man go, you are no friend of Caesar.'* (John 19:12, NIV.)

With this political weapon the Jewish priests scored a direct hit! Pilate's diplomatic record at HQ was not A1. Any further blunders could cost him his future.

To every man may come the moment when, like Pilate, he wants to do the right thing by Jesus, but finds himself among a minority in his favour and finally votes with a majority to defer any decision!

● **The inaction concerning Jesus that was desirable.** *'What shall I do?'*

Because an attitude of neutrality was now out of the question, Pilate sought to shift responsibility to others. In seeking various alternatives, Pilate sought to postpone the final decision in three ways:

Casualness. He tried to appear indifferent to the deeper issues involved and sought to delegate the verdict to the Jews; *' "Take him and judge him according to your law." '* It came back at him! *'The Jews said to him, "It is not lawful for us to put anyone to death." '* (John 18:31, RAV.)

Cowardice. *'Pilate sent Jesus to Herod.'* There was no love lost between the Roman governor and the puppet king, Herod Antipas. Pilate would not lift a finger to boost Herod's prestige but sought to dodge decision by playing on the King's vanity. We may not have a photocopy of the note

Pilate sent, but we can guess the content; 'Your Highness, This prisoner has been sent to me by your constituents. I realize that he comes under your jurisdiction and, of course, I should not dream of trespassing on your illustrious domain. . . . ' Pilate hoped that Herod might prove an escape route for him. It came back at him — again! *Herod treated Jesus with contempt . . . and sent him back to Pilate.*'

Cleverness. Pilate sought to engineer a situation which, his political acumen told him, would lead to the release of Jesus. He offered the people a choice which he thought would favour Jesus. There was a festival-custom that could come in useful. A prisoner was released at Passover every year by popular demand. That year's choice would be between a robber and a Rabbi. Apparently both had the same first name: Jesus-bar-Abbas and Jesus-bar-Joseph. Let the people decide. Logic and sentiment decreed the verdict would favour the Rabbi. But nothing can be more illogical and uncertain than public opinion. The 'pollsters' failed Pilate that day. It came back at him — again! *'Not this man, but Bar-Abbas.'* (John 18:40.)

● **The rejection of Christ that was incredible.** *'Behold the man.'*

Pilate had heard the evidence and examined the Accused.

He had reached a verdict; *'I find no fault in this man.'* Yet minutes later he sent the Prisoner to be crucified.

How could that happen?

The gospels provide the answer; *'Pilate, in his desire to satisfy the mob, released Barabas to them.'* (Mark 15:15, REB.) *'Their shouts prevailed.'* (Luke 23:23, REB.)

It is important to recognize the reason for Pilate's capitulation.

It was fear that chained him.

They had brought Jesus to Pilate in chains but, in fact, it was Pilate who was fettered. He was a coward.

But have *we* never been in bondage to what others might think or say about us?

Pilate was nearly finished with Jesus now. Just one more reaction. *'When Pilate saw that he could prevail nothing, but that rather a tumult was made, he took water, and washed his hands before the multitude.'* (Matthew 27:24.)

● **The farce that condemned Him.** *'I am innocent.'*

What did Pilate mean by these words? Was he admitting that Jesus was really the Judge and that he, Pilate, had been on trial? If Pilate was the *real* defendant, it was not water that was needed to absolve his guilt. . . . Not water, but blood, and that the very blood he was causing to be shed.

Years later it was written, *'The blood of Jesus Christ his Son cleanses us from all sin.'* (1 John 1:7, RAV.)

And that is what the cross of Christ was all about.

In the meantime we must stand alongside Pontius Pilate.

There are a variety of basins in which we may try to wash our hands.

Better that we take our hands out of the water and consider the most important question of all: *'What shall **I** do with Jesus?'*

Everything else is, in the ultimate, secondary to that question. Eternity hinges upon it. It is not, 'What shall I do with the church?'

Only *one* question matters.

> 'What will you do with Jesus,
> Neutral you cannot be.
> Some day your heart will be asking,
> What will He do with me?'

6 THE MARKS OF THE LORD JESUS

'I bear in my body the marks of the Lord Jesus,' wrote Paul in Galatians 6:17.

As a result of the persecutions Paul suffered, his statement was literally true (2 Corinthians 11:23-28).

But there is another sense in which it needs to be true for every Christian.

Unless Christian discipleship somehow displays a spiritual imprint of Calvary, it is unlikely that those uncommitted to the Christian Gospel will understand the significance of Christ's suffering.

What were the 'marks of the Lord Jesus'?

A crown made of the long-thorn briar was crushed on His head.

His hands and feet were spiked by Roman nails, square in section.

His side was riven by a soldier's spear.

We need to understand the 'wounds of Christ' in terms of daily Christian living. If 'believers' are part of the family of God it would seem logical that they should, at the very least, reflect some family resemblance to the Master.

• *'The soldiers twisted a thorny crown and put it on His head.'*

If you have handled a plait of 'thorny burnet' that grows wild in Jerusalem, you will have no doubt about the deep lacerations it would cause. But our attention need not be focused on the character of the wounds, but on the character of the One who was wounded. . . .

From the outset of His public ministry Jesus foresaw that His proclamation of the kingdom would lead to rejection and execution. (Mark 8:31.)

Nevertheless, *'He set His face steadfastly to go to Jerusalem'.* He had taught without compromise, challenged without fear, and given Himself without reserve.

Now, in response to a life of complete self-giving, they pierced His head with an emblem of regal mockery. His reaction is on record; *'Jesus gave no answer, not a single word.'*

So when we can come to the place of rejection or ridicule without becoming bitter or cynical, we shall bear in our body a mark of the Lord Jesus. It may be in the context of a family relationship that our response to God will be disputed. Perhaps in our business life our Christian witness will be discredited. Even in religious circles our motives may be misconstrued. . . .

The *head* is often spoken of as the 'seat of the intellect'. Does the passion of Christ in any way affect my intellectual reactions? Many a pastor who has sought to be reflectively honest about his faith and refused to compromise his loyalty to the ultimate authority of Scripture, has had to bear the 'thorny crown' of a dunce's cap and be labelled 'fundamentalist'! *'Let this mind be in you which was also in Christ Jesus'* . . . and hide your wounds in His.

● *'They pierced my hands and my feet.'* (Psalm 22:16.)

Human hands are essentially instruments of activity. With our hands we make and take, work and play. Rob a man of his hands and you negate his productive capacity.

Jesus knew all about crucifixion. At the time of His youth there had been a series of Zealot revolts in Palestine. The Romans had been ruthless in their reaction. Thousands of rebels had been crucified. And the crosses would have been visible along the road that went past Nazareth. . . . It was a public warning. Jesus knew the sickening truth about Roman reprisals.

But it is not the nature of crucifixion that demands our attention. It is the nature of the One crucified on a certain day at Golgotha, Jerusalem.

When we come to the place where our hands are 'tied' and we do not become impatient or enraged, we shall bear in our body a mark of the Lord Jesus. Our hands may be tied in various ways; family ties, restricting our freedom; financial ties, restricting our opportunities; educational ties, limiting our ambitions.

Jesus spent thirty years at home. He possessed little worldly wealth or capital. He received no 'university' recognition. However, because He let them take His hands then, He has the authority to take the whole world in His hands when He comes again. *'Behold! My hands and feet!'*

Human feet are primarily instruments of purpose and direction. They allow us freedom of movement to visit a friend or run from danger. Rob a man of his feet and you take away his mobility.

Yet the feet of Christ did not transport Him from Gethsemane when the traitor was preparing the betrayal. . . .

When we can come to the place of restriction and refuse to retreat. . . .

When we can meet inner fear without yielding to panic, and face physical pain with courage, we shall bear in our body a mark of the Lord Jesus.

There is a story of the early church in which Paul and Silas were imprisoned. *'He . . . fastened their feet in the stocks. . . . At midnight Paul and Silas were praying and singing hymns to God.'* (Acts 16:24, 25, RAV.) If, in a dark hour and a place of unwelcome confinement, we can find a reason to praise the Lord, others may recognize a mark of the Lord Jesus.

● *'One of the soldiers, with a spear, pierced his side.'*
Self-preservation is the strongest human instinct. Physical death is symbolic of spiritual disease . . . ; *'By one man sin entered into the world, and death by sin; and so death passed upon all men, for that all have sinned.'* (Romans 5:12.)

Only one man ever claimed immunity from that verdict, and that was Jesus. ' "*Which of you can convict me of sin? If what I say is true, why do you not believe me?*" ' (John 8:46, REB.)

We must come to terms with the challenge of Christ for *His resurrection is the vindication of all His claims.* Morally and spiritually, death had no claim on Jesus. He lived a perfect life, despite the pressure of every temptation, yet He chose to undergo the crisis of physical death. In a vital sense it was not crucifixion that killed Him. Jesus died of a broken heart.

From a medical point of view the words of John 19:34-36 are of special significance: '*One of the soldiers thrust a lance into his side, and at once there was a flow of blood and water. This is vouched for by an eyewitness, whose evidence is to be trusted. He knows that he speaks the truth, so that you too may believe; for this happened in fulfilment of the text of scripture: "No bone of his shall be broken."* ' (REB.)

Under extreme stress the rupture of the pericardium takes place. In this condition, the blood in the heart separates from the serum . . . ; 'blood and water'.

Listen as Jesus speaks to Pilate: ' "*You say that I am a king. For this I was born, and for this I have come into the world, to bear witness to the truth. Everyone who is of the truth hears my voice.*" ' (John 18:37, RSV.)

Jesus *chose* death, that through His risen life we might gain the promise of immortality.

His heart was broken on Calvary that His love might overflow through His redeemed community into all the world.

The cross becomes the victory sign for time and eternity. The message of the cross is one down the centuries and one across the world.

The kind of life Jesus lived, determined the kind of death He died. The kind of death Jesus died should determine the kind of life we lead.

His HEAD was pierced that we might bear the Mark of His HUMILITY.

His HANDS were pierced that we might bear the Mark of His PATIENCE.

His FEET were pierced that we might bear the Mark of His OBEDIENCE.

His HEART was pierced that we might bear the Mark of His LOVE.

7 THE GOSPEL IN SEVEN WORDS

Jesus Christ is the central figure in Scripture.

The cross is its central symbol. All Scripture, and (according to Scripture) all history, lie beneath its shadow.

Paul declared that while the preaching of the cross was a stumbling block to Jews and foolishness to Gentiles, it is the *'power of God to save them'*. (1 Corinthians 1:23, 24, LB.)

There are many facets to the truth of the crucifixion. If we seek to consider any one single aspect of Calvary we may — so to speak — be unable to see the wood for the Tree.

We hold out not a crucifix but an empty cross. Therefore we ponder again the living words that have echoed from Golgotha down the arches of twenty centuries.

1. ' *"Father, forgive them, for they do not know what they do."* ' (Luke 23:34, RAV.)

During His earthly ministry Jesus spoke from many different pulpits. From a boat on the lake. From a mountainside. In an upper room. In the courts of the temple. Finally He spoke from the cross. It was reserved to the last for Him to occupy the 'ultimate in pulpits'.

From the statement *'Father forgive'*, the early teaching delivered in Galilee was demonstrated at Calvary. In His sermons Jesus had taught forgiveness; *'Pray for your enemies.'* Simon Peter asked: *'How often shall I forgive?'* Jesus replied: *'Until seventy times seven.'*

Now it is not the way of nature to forgive. Ask the tiger to give up its prey. Ask the avalanche to spare the climber. Ask the storm to pity the sailor. Nature's laws seem inexorable.

Again, it is not natural for *human nature* to forgive. Society has a built-in resistance. Ask the mother of an abused child. Look down the ages and see how revenge has burnt its way into history. Listen to the blinded Samson; *'God, give me strength that I may be avenged of my two eyes.'*

In stark contrast, the first word from Calvary was a prayer for forgiveness. Jesus prayed for those who had just laid down their hammers! Yet this word is more than a prayer; it is a plea. *'Father, they do not know what they do.'*

Blindness was their trouble. Enlightenment was their need.

The prodigal did not know what he did when he squandered his legacy. When he *'came to himself'* he turned for home.

Judas did not know what he did when he took the thirty pieces of silver. When the truth dawned he went and hanged himself. How dark was the world? Are we still in the dark? Maybe, but light has come. Once in history Christ walked the earth. For our salvation — love spoke from the cross.

We can no longer taunt heaven that darkness is our portion. As a film exposed to the sun is never the same again, but ever after must reveal the record of its encounter with light, so, if we have listened to the voice of Jesus, we cannot forget the truth He has uttered. *'This is the condemnation,'* says the fourth gospel, *'that light is come into the world, and men loved darkness rather than light'.* (John 3:19.)

In the light of the first word from the cross, our human dilemma is that we have no excuse.

2. *'And Jesus said to him, "Assuredly, I say to you today: you will be with me in paradise." '* (Luke 23:43, RAV.)

During His ministry Jesus had all kinds of friends. There were times when His disciples felt He ought to be more selective. Children took too much of His time. He talked with people like the woman of Samaria. His concern for some social outcast brought critical comment; *'This man receives sinners and eats with them.'* It is clear that Jesus was a great mixer, but never did He find Himself in such wretched company as in the hour of His death. *'They crucified him between two thieves.'* He who was sinless and had come to save sinners was to spend His last moments between two terrorists.

Isaiah's Messianic prophecy was precise; *'He was numbered with the transgressors.'*

During His ministry Jesus had all kinds of followers. Fishermen and tax men, Zealots and centurions, high and low, rich and poor. He was the perfect Friend, and His approach drew the best out of others. Jesus saw men not misshapen as they were, but in terms of what they might become. Nothing was more real to Jesus than human potential.

Suddenly, on the cross, there was a shape of things to come in the homage of a dying victim; *'Lord, remember me when you come into your kingdom.'* In relation to human personality we cannot define the parts played by conscience and reason when they are free to operate.

We cannot dogmatize in many matters relating to time and eternity. Yet, in the case of this dying man, maybe we can surmise:

Every kingdom, he may have reasoned, has its rulers. In the realm beyond, who will be sovereign? Not those who make others stepping stones for selfish ends. Not the dictators of this world. Why not this Man who has been 'set up' by his enemies? This Man who has prayed for His destroyers?

When a man sees the moral stature of Jesus he is not far from the kingdom. *'Lord, remember me.' In extremis* he cannot look beyond human disaster. On the verge of eternity it was revealed that Jesus is the One to whom every knee shall bow. During His ministry Jesus had said: *'Whoever comes to me I will in no wise cast out.'* That promise was made in Galilee. Now, at Calvary, the offer was put to the test. Was there room in paradise for a gangster? The Master knew.

3. ' *"Woman, behold your son!"* . . . *"Behold your mother!"* ' (John 19:26, 27, RAV.)

If you look closely at life you will see that it is woven in two-ply. One strand of our own choosing, the other strand not of our choice at all! When we are young we only consider one strand. Life is to be ours. We shall plan the pattern. Select the thread. Choose the colours. It will be all our own work!

As the years go by we discover we are not as free as we had imagined. We have to adapt the pattern, accept other threads, use different colours. We have the task of making something out of the two-ply of *choice* and *circumstance.*

Long ago there was a bright-eyed maiden in Nazareth full of the shining expectancy of youth. Then, in a moment, the simple pattern of her life became complicated. She had to take into her life another strand. She was called to take a leading part in God's plan for the ages. She was asked to be the mother of the Messiah. An angel said, ' "*The Holy Spirit will come upon you, . . . the holy child to be born will be called Son of God.*" ' How did Mary answer? ' "*I am the Lord's servant, may it be as you have said.*" '

Many Old Testament prophets shrank from a divine commission. Moses made excuses. Jonah took a sea cruise as an escape route. Isaiah wailed, '*Woe is me.*'

Mary took no evasive action. ' "*I am here*", she said, "*to serve the Lord.*" ' (Luke 1:38, Moffatt.)

How many times did Mary have to repeat those words? There were bitter misunderstandings in the early months . . . the hassle that came with the birth . . . the threats that disrupted the infancy. Later on, what anxieties must have encompassed Mary as Jesus came to manhood!

Mary is not associated with tight-lipped stoicism. But we *do* see her advancing with confidence in the divine purpose and sense of wonder at being God's instrument.

Now, at Calvary . . . the prophecy of old Simeon was being fulfilled . . . '*A sword shall pierce your own soul.*' Still she was standing by. . . . Could she still say, 'I am here to serve the Lord'?

'*When Jesus saw His mother.*' He was looking at the one who had first taught Him the Scriptures and heard Him memorizing the passages that later undergirded His ministry.

'*When Jesus saw His mother.*' He saw the one who brought Him on His first visit to Jerusalem before Joseph had died.

Jesus knew the hardships of widowhood. How graciously He had praised the widow's mite! How gladly He removed the cup of sorrow from the widow of Nain and restored her son!

But now, by bitter irony, the Widow of Nazareth was to suffer the very thing the widow of Nain had been spared.

Son of God and Son of Mary: He had to weave something out of that two-ply; to face the temporal and the eternal and make the right decision about both. With tender and practical foresight Jesus commended Mary to the one beloved disciple who was brave enough to stand at the cross.

God grant that we may say with Mary, '*I am here to serve the Lord.*'

God grant that we may never lose a 'family concern' for those who carry the weight of the cross on their hearts.

4. ' "*My God, my God, why have you forsaken me?*" ' (Matthew 27:46, RAV.)

If there is one 'last word' that needs cautious comment, this is it. We must take off our shoes before we open our mouths. . . .

John Milton wrote a poem on the birth of Jesus and later started to write a companion work on the death of Jesus. He did not succeed. There was a fragment of verse, but it seems that, finding the subject beyond him, the author left it unfinished.

Three hours intervened between the third and fourth words from the cross. The beloved disciple had led away the sorrowing mother. Many of the spectators had wandered away. There are limits even to the morbid curiosity of a mob.

There had been less drama at the execution than the rabble had anticipated. No denunciation on the wagging heads that railed against the Sufferer. No call for fire from heaven to consume them. No miraculous intervention.

Nothing. Nothing — save agony borne with majestic calm, with a prayer for pardon, and with a promise to the penitent.

In vain they had tried to provoke something more spectacular. 'Come down, and we'll believe!' But the only answer was the darkening sky and the passing of time.

Suddenly that cry . . . 'My God, WHY?'

Many commentators have sought to answer and explain.

Peter wrote that he bore *'our sins in his own body on the tree'.* (1 Peter 2:24, RAV.) That truth reveals the heart of the Gospel though the human mind cannot fathom its depths.

We may be unable to grasp the full significance of this fourth word from Calvary, but there is a clue if we consider the context of the cry. . . .

How many accounts of the crucifixion are there in the Bible?

Four?

Or are there *five?*

Read Psalm 22:1-18. Surely, these words relate to Calvary. They were written centuries before the birth of Jesus, but they prefigure the redemptive work of the Messiah. Christ's life and ministry were influenced by the prophecies of Scripture. At every crisis point he found guidance and assurance in the Word. Suppose at this final 'flash point' Jesus was facing the reality of prophecy? Is it possible that through the 'window' of this Psalm we are permitted to see how the Lord grappled with and overthrew the adversary?

This may not answer all our questions, but it gives a reverent assessment on that cry. We need this perspective, for we too are vulnerable. Not to the anguish of redemption the Lord knew. But to those encounters with sorrow, pain and bereavement that are the universal lot of man.

At times of testing there may seem to be no middle road between despair and faith. Happy the soul that, in such circumstances, can fall back with certainty upon the promises of Scripture and can look to Him, *'who for the joy that was set before him endured the cross, despising the shame, and has sat down at the right hand of the throne of God'.* (Hebrews 12:2, RAV.)

5. *'I thirst.'* (John 19:28.)

Jesus was often questioned about life's priorities. His answers left no room for doubt; *'Thou shalt love the Lord thy God . . . and thy neighbour as thyself.'* On these priorities Jesus built the ethic that was primary. This fifth word from the cross registers awful pain that climaxed in an intolerable thirst. While it would serve no major purpose to descend into a clinical description of the crucifixion, this word would have been significant to many of the first readers of the fourth gospel. About that time the young church was endangered by false teachers: Gnostics.

One tenet of Gnosticism was that spirit is all good and matter is all evil. Their conclusion was that God could never inhabit a body because body is matter and therefore evil. They went on to argue that God cannot suffer, so Jesus did not suffer pain! These Gnostics believed they were honouring God and Jesus. In fact, they were destroying Jesus.

If God were to redeem man, He must *become* man.

His agony of thirst was a mark of His full humanity.

In varying degrees pain is universal. . . .

'The whole creation groans and travails in pain together. . . .'

We have to wrestle with that problem. When pain strikes we are less than mature if we protest, 'Why should it happen to me?' Who are we to claim exemption?

On the other hand we should not wax sentimental about the sum of the world's pain. Pain is not cumulative. A thousand people in pain are not in more pain than one person.

On the cross Jesus was not too proud to let the soldiers know His pain and allow one of them to show pity. People who suffer tight-lipped, exulting in a stoical display have not been taught by Jesus who was as open in admitting pain as He was heroic in bearing it.

Pain and suffering were never in God's creative will.

If God ordained suffering then dedicated doctors and nurses are obstructing the divine purpose! All the healing miracles of Jesus testify that pain and disease ought to be cast out. That Roman soldier who lifted the sponge to the Master's lips was typical of all who seek to assuage the world's pain.

The figure on the cross who accepted the suffering put his seal on all such actions.

Two questions trouble a suffering humanity: 'Does God understand?' and 'Does God care?'

The Christ of Calvary says, 'I thirst,' and shows he understands. . . .

The Christ of Olivet says, *'All power is given unto me. . . . Go ye. . . .'*

We are to go, because He cares.

6. *'It is finished.'* (John 19:30.)

You can tell a good craftsman by the quality of his work and his attention to detail. It is unlikely that shoddy items came out of the workshop at Nazareth. We are told that Jesus wore a special robe 'woven in one piece, without seam'. Perhaps Mary made it, fashioned it by her love and skill. Even the soldiers were impressed, and in the end rather than dissect it — they diced for it!

It is easier to put a finishing touch on a piece of wood or fabric than to put a mark of perfection on a life! But Jesus did. Like a seamless robe His whole life from Bethlehem to Calvary was all of one piece. There were no seams or patches or tattered edges. Even Pilate had to say, *'I find no fault in him.'*

Now Jesus had reached the end of life's road. The conflict was nearly over. And what did He say?

'It is accomplished. . . .' It is a word of completion and triumph. In human terms he was 'cut off in the prime of life', but He had done all He had set out to do. Life is not just a number of years. It is not what life does to

you, but what you do with life that matters. Judged by this standard His life was complete.

In those hours of darkness, evil was making its fiercest assault. . . .

Below Him voices uttered subtle persuasions. . . . *'If thou be the Son of God, come down.'*

They *might* have believed for a little while if He had come down. But the centuries have believed in Him because He stayed up!

We hail Him as Lord because He went through to the finish.

At Golgotha men whispered, 'He's finished.' But Jesus cried with a loud voice, *'It is finished.'*

There is a hymn that sums it up:

'He died that we might be forgiven' — we have been saved from the *penalty* of sin.

'He died to make us good' — we are being saved from the *power* of sin.

'That we might go at last to heaven' — we shall be saved from the *presence* of sin.

There are those who call such conviction presumption. In the light of the sixth word from Calvary it is *redemption*.

7. *'Father, into thy hands I commend my spirit.'* (Luke 23:46.)

This last word from the cross might seem an anti-climax.

Agony and anguish are passed. We are given certainty and serenity compressed into eight words.

Like the first word, it is a prayer. But not an original one. It comes from Psalm 31:5 and it was a goodnight prayer a Jewish mother taught her child. Jesus learned it at Mary's knee and now He adds the word ABBA (Father). This is not a sad prayer, but it is a solemn one. Life is an adventure, but living is a fatal disease. *'Therefore, just as through one man sin entered the world, and death through sin, and*

thus death spread to all men, because all sinned . . . .'
(Roman 5:12, RAV.)

Death is generally the last subject people discuss because many are afraid. And not without reason. Despite the sophistication of our 'funeral parlours' death is still THE LAST ENEMY.

The Good News is that, *'For as in Adam all die, even so in Christ all shall be made alive. But each one in his own order.'* (1 Corinthians 15:22, 23, RAV.)

If Jesus is our Elder Brother we ought to be comforted by the simplicity of His death. There is another old hymn that puts things plainly:

'Teach me to live that I may dread

The grave as little as my bed.'

As a sinful mortal I could have no hope beyond the grave.

The resurrection of Jesus Christ is the only hope and pledge that when He comes again *'this mortal shall put on immortality'.*

Because of the cross of Calvary my hope is not for a solemn requiem, but for a Saviour's return.

8 JOSEPH OF ARIMATHEA:
The case of the committed councillor

The Apostle Paul wrote, '*Not many wise, . . . not many mighty, not many noble, are called.*' (1 Corinthians 1:26, RAV.) Surprising, then, that Joseph of Arimathea, without doubt one of the wise and notable, is rather under-written by the New Testament authors. The gospel writers present just fragments:

● **Matthew** — tells simply that Joseph was '*a rich man from Arimathea*'. There is a certain humorous logic in the fact that it took the ex-tax inspector, Levi Matthew, to note Joseph's bank balance and home address! Then, in a spirit of fellowship, Matthew adds that Joseph '*had also become a disciple of Jesus*'. (27:57, RAV.)

● **Mark** — describes Joseph as '*a prominent council member.*' (15:43, RAV.) This designation has interesting over-tones. The more so since it is recorded of Joseph that he was a '*Noblis Decurio*'. *Decurio* was a recognized office in the Roman Empire. Cicero had a favourite villa in Pompeii. At that time its city council consisted of *Decurios*, who had been magistrates. They were so important that, with a certain irony, Cicero complained that it was easier to become a Senator of Rome than a *Decurio* in Pompeii! Mark adds that Joseph was '*eagerly expecting the arrival of God's Kingdom*'. (LB.)

● **Luke** — introduces Joseph as '*a member of the Council*'. (23:50, 51, NEB.) This Council — the Sanhedrin — was the supreme Council and high court at Jerusalem. Luke adds that Joseph was '*a good upright man*' and, as if to amplify his verdict, further states, '*Who had dissented from their policy and the action they had taken.*' Luke qualifies Mark's comment on Joseph's vision of the kingdom with the phrase, *'Who had been expecting the Messiah's coming.'* (LB.)

● **John** — confirms Joseph as being *'a disciple of Jesus, but secretly, for fear of the Jews'.* (19:38, RAV.) This need not imply cowardice. It *could* indicate that at that time of political and religious unrest Joseph reasoned he could serve his Master (and possibly kinsmen) best by maintaining a low profile.

Here, then, was Joseph of Arimathea. A man of substance and status. A man of moral integrity in relation to Jewish law, and of spiritual vitality regarding messianic scriptures. As a disciple of Jesus he had opened his mind to the Master's teaching and to the 'signs' that accompanied His ministry.

After his involvement with Pontius Pilate and the death of Jesus, Joseph of Arimathea disappears from the scene. An ancient manuscript in the Vatican narrates that he was expelled from the Sanhedrin and banished from his homeland in the dispersion of the apostles that followed the martyrdom of Stephen.

First-century Christians were often unpopular because of their positive beliefs. At the end of the twentieth century it is often the case that Christians are unpopular because of their negative attitudes. Believers do not honour God by becoming brash in their demonstrations of faith. The secular world reacts violently against the sort of pietism that makes a high profession but exhibits a low performance. *'But even if you should suffer for righteousness' sake, you are blessed.'* (1 Peter 3:14, RAV.)

If we want to know how the winds of unpopularity can arise, the story of Joseph of Arimathea is instructive. His involvement with the events of the Gospel deepened when he discarded the cloak of formal association with Jesus to identify himself with the crucified Christ. Although the gospels are not specific, it would seem that Joseph was himself an observer of the events at Golgotha and was aware of the moment of Christ's death. The more we ponder the remarkable action of Joseph following the death of Jesus, the less we are able to attribute it solely to factors like personal courage and social convention. . . .

Isaiah's fifty-third chapter has been described, by some, as a 'hidden' and 'forbidden' passage. Certainly it contains a vivid prophecy of the 'Suffering Servant' Messiah which, for Orthodox Jewry, is still too hot to handle. Had Joseph's mind been enlightened to the reality of the prophetic phrases of Isaiah 53? Was it at Golgotha that the conviction took hold of him that Jesus was, in fact, the 'Anointed Christ'?

'*He was despised, shunned by all, pain-racked and afflicted by disease; we despised him, we held him of no account, an object from which people turn away their eyes. Yet it was our afflictions he was bearing, our pain he endured, while we thought of him as smitten by God, . . . But he was pierced for our transgressions, crushed for our iniquities; the chastisement he bore restored us to health and by his wounds we are healed.*' (Isaiah 53:3-5, REB.)

If Joseph had, in fact, absorbed this truth it can be asserted that he was the first 'fulfilled Jew' and, with Nicodemus, was '*born again to a living hope*'. (1 Peter 1:3, NAS.)

At the human level, when Joseph made his decision he faced several types of unpopularity:

● **Joseph risked national enmity;** Joseph went '*boldly to Pilate*' (Mark 15:43, RAV.) Some have said that family connections prompted Joseph's request of Pilate. But it would take more than 'family connections' to overcome his ingrained Jewish antipathy to the Roman Governor. As well as being Caesar's agent, Pilate's personal disregard of Jewish religious scruples made him a detested man in Israel. Jews were fiercely nationalistic, and any member of their Sanhedrin who engaged in personal, private negotiation with Pilate was bound to face suspicion, perhaps ostracism.

Christians must seek a patriotism that is higher than

nationalism. It is natural and right to honour the land of one's birth. But Jesus died to redeem racialism by His own universal sovereignty. No Christian should say, 'My country — right or wrong.' We must not seek peace at any price, but righteousness at any cost. And that may involve a willingness to challenge corruption in our own society.

● **Joseph risked social hostility;** Joseph *'begged the body of Jesus'*. And this action invited double-trouble for Joseph. In biblical times anyone who involved themselves with a condemned man could be identified with the crime of the accused.

Consider the nature of the charges levelled at Jesus. His disciples knew *they* were under suspicion; *'the doors were shut where the disciples were assembled, for fear of the Jews.'* (John 20:19, RAV.)

Whatever grounds Joseph may have had for seeking custody of the Lord's body, it would certainly lead to censure by the Sanhedrin. It is easy to say, 'I don't care what others think and do.' But it is rarely true. Man is a social animal. Being cold-shouldered by his associates is a price that he would do a great deal to avoid paying.

'Then he took it (the body) down' from the cross. (Luke 23:53, RAV.) Impressive words! When Pilate had acceded to his request, Joseph of Arimathea went back to Golgotha himself and, in a crowd situation charged with unusual tension, he supervised the task that had to be undertaken. This was courage of the highest order.

An unpredictable element in human nature often manifests itself in a crowd-reaction. Normally quiet and unassuming people will say and do things *en masse* which they would never contemplate individually. In the emotionally-charged atmosphere of civil unrest, a single word or signal can spark off mob violence. Today's climate of public opinion is volatile. Once respected in the West, the Church is now just tolerated. This tolerance is a byproduct of social apathy. But social apathy could change to quite a different reaction as quickly as the wind. If a church true to its mission could prick the conscience of the nation, then the smile of tolerance could quickly turn to the snarl of hostility.

● **Joseph risked religious penalty;** *'They took the body of Jesus and following Jewish burial customs they wrapped it, with the spices, in strips of linen cloth.'* (John 19:40, REV.)

The Jews had strict rules about death. Apart from the *mode* of burial there were other ceremonial laws. (Numbers 19:11-16.)

For Joseph to act as undertaker on the Eve of Passover — and *for one condemned to death for blasphemy* — must in orthodox terms have represented the ultimate of the unthinkable!

Joseph had been caught up in a system that considered outward observance of religious regulations to be of primary importance. Any deviation from tradition and you were anathema!

This is still a curse in much institutional religion.

Let a man do this . . . he is a Catholic. Let a man *not* do that . . . he is a Protestant. Let him say this . . . he is labelled a 'Modernist'. Let him say that . . . he is labelled 'Fundamentalist'.

Thus emerges the stereotype cleric whose main aim appears to be acceptance in the right ecclesiastical circle or, on the other hand, to be rated among the doctrinal elite.

Such clerics would have little in common with Joseph of Arimathea.

The Church must have sound doctrine and clear discipline. But it must be the doctrine of Christ and the discipline of Christ's Spirit. Love grows soft if it is not strengthened by truth, and truth grows hard if it is not softened by love.

'When Joseph had taken the body, he . . . laid it in his new tomb. . . .' (Matthew 27:59, 60, RAV.)

Could Joseph have fully realized what he was doing?

Jesus Christ died the death of a common criminal. Such an execution usually meant that the victim had no decent burial. Yet Joseph and Nicodemus provided a burial fit for a King! Somebody once commented that you would need an advanced computer to work out the ratio of probability that a crucified criminal would be given a 'royal' burial! But it had all been prophesied; *'He was buried like a criminal in a rich man's grave; but he had done no wrong.'* (Isaiah 53:9, LB.)

A young agnostic student once propounded the theory that Jesus was a 'freak' of history. He argued that, as Mozart was to music, and Einstein was to science, so Jesus was to religion — a genius. Such a notion is fatally flawed. The arrival of neither Mozart nor Einstein was predicted in the course of history. By contrast, no one can understand the Person of Jesus Christ until they have studied the biblical prophecies concerning Messiah. The truth about Jesus Christ is revealed in the fact that every prophecy concerning the first advent of Messiah was fulfilled in His birth-life-teaching-and-death.

That student's Mozart-Einstein parallel does *not* work as an assessment of Jesus.

It is a stab at a neutral verdict.

Jesus does not offer the option of neutrality.

C. S. Lewis said it like this: 'I'm trying to prevent anyone saying the really foolish thing that people often say about Him: "I am ready to accept Jesus as a great moral Teacher, but I don't accept His claim to be God." That is the one thing we must not say. A man who was merely a man and said the sort of things Jesus said would not be a great moral teacher. He would either be a lunatic — on a level with a man who says he is a poached egg — or else he would be the devil. You must make your choice. Either this man was, and is the Son of God: or else a madman or something worse. . . .'

You can shut Him up for a fool. You can spit at Him as a demon. Or you can fall at His feet and call Him Lord and God.

But let us not come with any patronizing nonsense about His being simply 'a great human teacher'. He has not left that option open to us. He never intended to.

9 NICODEMUS:
The case of the curious cleric

'There was a man of the Pharisees named Nicodemus. . . . '
(John 3:1.)

The background of John 3 hints that this Jewish religious leader had been commissioned by his colleagues to investigate Jesus of Nazareth.

Jesus was creating something of a sensation among the population at large. Two factors had focused attention on Him. First, John the Baptist's assessment that the ministry of Jesus superseded his own. Second, the appearance of Jesus in Jerusalem where he denounced priests and Scribes and expelled from the temple precincts those who were turning the Court of the Holy Place into an unholy market.

'Who is this?' the people wanted to know. 'Who does he think he is?' echoed the priests. So they delegated a professor of theology to find out. . . .

Who *was* Nicodemus?

Some facts are clear from the gospels. He was a Pharisee. A ruler of the Jews. A member of the Sanhedrin, which was a convocation of seventy-two men and very much the 'inner cabinet' of Jewish national affairs. As well as being a man with a certain political acumen, he was also a thought-leader in matters spiritual. When Jesus asked him, 'Are you a master in Israel?' it implied that Nicodemus was a top theologian. Versed in Scripture and conversant with all the sacred writings of the Jews, Nicodemus probably appeared the ideal person to investigate the tiresome case of Jesus of Nazareth.

But Nicodemus was in for a surprise and about to encounter a dimension of spiritual authority previously outside his experience. This was apparent as soon as they met. Their encounter was at night. We are not told the location.

Nevertheless we can be fairly sure that it was somewhere on the Mount of Olives.

The interesting thing about this evening interview is the impact of Jesus upon his interrogator.

The story unfolds like a stage drama.

● *'You must be born again.'* (See verse 3.) This was Jesus' opener. And what an opener! Nicodemus, educated, cultured, intelligent, an advanced thinker in theological matters, must have found himself unnerved. As with present-day ecclesiastics, Nicodemus may have thought that the 'new birth' imperative applied to people of uncertain morality and low IQ. Nicodemus was no 'publican' or 'sinner' but evidently the new birth imperative applied also to notable academics!

On the defensive, Nicodemus asked: *'How can these things be?'*

Jesus powered on; *'Except a man be born of water and of the Spirit, he cannot enter into the kingdom.'* (Verse 5.) This was not necessarily a reference to baptism. Both Jesus and Nicodemus related the concept to the facts of childbirth. The provisions of nature, from conception to birth, include an amniotic sac containing the fluid in the womb which, when the time comes, breaks and makes the baby's delivery easier. 'Born of the water' was how rabbinical writings referred to this process. Nicodemus understood this. Jesus was guiding him to a new dimension of truth. Nicodemus was being taught that it is possible to have a religious profession without a spiritual possession.

Why the new birth imperative?

Because a man is spiritually blind; *'Except a man be born again he cannot see. . . .'* (Verse 3.) Paul, who moved among intellectuals, accepted this truth; *'The natural man does not receive the things of God, because they are spiritually discerned.'* Secular culture is often a barrier to vital faith. Agnostic reasoning and human rationalism are like sundials: only reliable if rightly related to the 'Son'! Spiritual blindness comes with the 'fallen creature' status of man; because of this infirmity his mind is as fatally flawed as his other faculties.

- *'Unless one is born of water and the Spirit, he cannot enter. . . .'* (Verse 5, RAV.)

Self-seeking and self-righteousness are endemic to human nature. Hence man becomes imprisoned in his own philosophies. New birth is an imperative because, until man's pride and prejudice yield to divine revelation, he cannot see, and is not free to respond, to God.

What is the nature of this new birth?

Nicodemus was familiar with the 'new birth' concept but, on the defensive, posed his question in an obtuse way: *'How can a man be born when he is old?'* (Verse 4.) The most positive construction that we can place upon his question is that he was anxious to know more of the nature of new birth. His academic background had taught him the concept, but he needed to move from the shadow to the substance. He needed to break out of the narrow confines of materialistic thought. Adopting his mood Jesus asked him, 'Are you a teacher of Israel and yet you do not understand this?'

So how *can* a man be born again?

A Saviour makes it possible: 'As Moses lifted up the serpent in the wilderness, even so must the Son of Man be lifted up. . . .' (Verse 14.) Jesus takes Nicodemus back to his own study source in the book of Numbers (21:9). The Israelites were in a dangerous wilderness situation. Bitten by serpents, in danger of death from venom, there was life in a look. Moses lifted aloft a brazen serpent on a banner-staff. And the banner-staff was shaped like a cross. 'Even so,' Jesus told Nicodemus, 'the Son of Man must be lifted up. . . .' There was life in a look in the wilderness; there would be life in a look at the crucified One. And this lifting up would be the key to the restored relationship between God and man, the means of man's salvation.

The Spirit makes it practical: ' *"The wind blows where it wills; you hear the sound of it, but you do not know where it comes from or where it is going. So it is with everyone who is born from the Spirit."* ' (Verse 8, REB.) As this evening conversation developed, Jesus drew a parable from the night breeze. He was saying to Nicodemus, 'You may be a learned academic, but with all your scholarship you cannot dictate to the Spirit of God.' New birth brings a revelation of truth, a sweet reasonableness even in things that might previously have seemed unreasonable. New birth brings a revelation of purpose, a new meaningfulness in things that once seemed unprofitable.

The surrender makes it personal: ' *"Everyone who has faith may in him have eternal life."* ' (Verse 15, REB.) New birth is not a process of brainwashing. It is the response of faith to the person and prompting of Christ.

• *'One of their number, Nicodemus (the man who once visited Jesus), intervened. "Does our law",* he asked them, *"permit us to pass judgement on someone without first giving him a hearing and learning the facts?"* ' (John 7:50, 51, REB.)

Here we find Nicodemus commending Jesus.

Another controversy in Jerusalem. This time, in the midst of the Jewish Feast of Tabernacles (John 7:11-36). Every day for a week there had been services and festivities. Pomp, procession and ritual. Water from the Pool of Siloam had been poured over the temple altar. In a land where water is life, it was a thanksgiving for rain and rivers. But it was more, far more than that. This became evident when, at the climax of the Festival on 'the Sabbath of the Great Hosanna', Jesus strode purposefully to the centre of the vast crowd covering Temple Mount — and probably the hills and valleys around — and proclaimed: *'If anyone is thirsty, let him come to me and drink.'* (Verse 37, REB.)

Imagine the sensation.

The chief priests were furious. At the peak moment the ritual had been interrupted. The temple police were sent for to arrest Jesus.

In special session there was confusion in the Sanhedrin (verses 40-48). If ever there was a meeting governed by fury and hate, it was that assembly.

But of the seventy-two men present, Nicodemus stood out. Dumbfounded, the temple police had sat listening to Jesus. No attempt had been made to arrest Him. When the Sanhedrin asked why, the militia responded: *'No one ever spoke as this man speaks.'* (Verse 46, REB.) Building on their testimony Nicodemus defied the mood of the meeting. He demanded that before passing judgement the facts of the case should be ascertained, and Jesus should be given a hearing.

The man who first came to Jesus by night was beginning to come out into the light! The Sanhedrin were quick with their retort; ' *"Are you a Galilean too?"* ' (Verse 52, REB.) Nicodemus soon found out what it cost to be a disciple.

Nicodemus is often spoken of as 'a secret disciple'. However, when he spoke up it was to register a claim for justice. And if ever a man was qualified to register such a claim, that man was Nicodemus. He referred 'learned council' to a principle of law they knew well. (Deuteronomy 1:17.) When, in our presence, men decry God and His Gospel, do they receive a clear testimony to indicate where we stand?

There is a growing antipathy to the Gospel in some parts of our society. There is even a 'God is dead' school of modern theology! And from there on down, there are other schools from ultra-high, to high, to moderately high. . . . Professor Edwyn Hoskyns once said, 'Oh! The accursed theologians who, instead of being on their knees at the cross, are sitting on the throne of God posing critical questions!

When once theology loses its humility, consign it to the dustbin.'

● *'Nicodemus brought a mixture of myrrh and aloes . . . .'* (John 19:39, NIV.)

True devotion is most clearly demonstrated in adverse circumstances.

Jesus had been executed as a criminal. Nevertheless, the faith of Nicodemus shone brightest when the main company of Christ's disciples had retreated.

He who came first to Jesus by night was last to leave when the sun set on Golgotha.

This man's dedication was expressed in unsparing devotion and undaunted discipleship. John's gospel tells us that the burial ointment that Nicodemus brought was *'a mixture of myrrh and aloes, about a hundred pounds weight'*.

Some Bible commentators query this. 'Obvious error,' say some. 'Quite excessive,' write others.

Perhaps the amount was more *expressive* than excessive!

Nicodemus poured out his suppressed allegiance in unsparing fashion.

There is high drama behind the story of Christ's burial. Apart from Joseph of Arimathea, here was a 'Master of Israel' disqualifying himself from participation in the Passover festival by assisting in the burial of a man executed for blasphemy. Nicodemus was so convinced in his mind as to the significance of the events on Golgotha that no task, however uncongenial, could deter his response.

Jesus had said, *'If any man will be my disciple, let him take up his cross. . . .'* Nicodemus was ready to take up his cross now. He did more: he took up the Christ of the cross.

Maybe the truth of his first conversation with Jesus had dawned on his soul; *'As Moses lifted up the serpent in the wilderness, even so must the Son of man be lifted up.'* (John 3:14.)

At the moment when it seemed that Jesus was discredited

and defeated, Nicodemus brought an offering worthy of Messiah.

We look back on this event from the comfortable pew of a respectable church. It wasn't like that for Nicodemus. He had occupied an uncomfortable seat in a hostile assembly that had voted to kill the Son of God! There is no record of what happened to Nicodemus. The New Testament does not mention him again. Perhaps it is sufficient for us to know that the curious cleric became a committed Christian.

10 ENCOUNTER WITH 'THE GARDENER'

'Supposing him to be the gardener . . . ' (John 20:15, RAV.)
It would be hard to find a more placid phrase to describe
the most astounding incident in history.

This sentence occurs in the poignant account of a woman
so dazed and distracted with grief that she made a great mistake. She met God. But she mistook Him for a gardener!

Perhaps it is not as illogical as it sounds.

Joseph of Arimathea had supervised the burial of Jesus.
His gardener would certainly have assisted. Mary Magdalene
had observed the preparation of the tomb. So, what more
likely person to be in the Garden shortly after sunrise than
the gardener?

We accept that Mary spoke while under a misapprehen-
sion. But there are lessons to be learned from her confusion.
In a vital sense, Jesus Christ is the Gardener of human lives.
That assumption promotes important considerations.

● **It is the hand of the gardener that plants.** A basic
tenet of the Christian faith is that God has a purpose for the
lives of His people. We are not particles of fatalistic flotsam
drifting on the ocean of time. We are seeds planted in the
soil of a Creator's allotment.

The act of planting involves the vision of an end product.

Firstly, there is the principle of selection. A skilled gardener will choose soil best suited to the genus of the plant.
He will seek a place in the garden where the plant is most
likely to take root. Whether in sunshine or shadow, the wisdom of the gardener seeks to guide the planting. Too often
in life it is rebellion against circumstances that leads to stunted
growth. In one of his letters (Philippians 4:11) Paul wrote: *'I
have learned, in whatsoever state I am, therewith to be con-*

tent.' That was not dull resignation. It was a conviction that the ground of faith is always fertile with spiritual possibility.

Secondly, there is the principle of separation. Seedlings are packed tightly together in the early days of growth. But they would never come to maturity if they remained in a 'hothouse' situation. Hence the gardener separates and plants them out to stimulate development.

Fellowship is a necessity for young believers. But we should not be surprised if, as we begin to grow spiritually, we are placed in a situation where we have to depend less on others, and put down deeper roots of our own. The hand of the Gardener may transplant us to a new area of growth that would have been retarded in a 'nursery environment'.

There is a vivid illustration of this in the story in Acts 8. *'The angel of the Lord said to Philip, Arise . . . go to Gaza . . . which is desert.'* It must have seemed illogical to Philip to be called away from a demanding mission in Samaria to serve in the desert. How frustrating to leave a city campaign for a wilderness excursion! Philip did not know that an Ethiopian ambassador was travelling in that desert! He might have procrastinated. But he did not. The hand that planted him in a place of seeming isolation was using him to sow the seed of redemption that was carried by the wind of the Spirit into the heart of the African continent.

Ethiopia has a history of Christian influence dating from the first century. We may well trace this back to the servant of Christ who was willing to accept the challenge of the Master's transplantation.

● **It is the hand of the gardener that prunes.** Whether it is among the flowers or the fruit trees, there comes a time when the gardener's hand must hold a knife.

If the rose is to bloom to perfection, or the tree to yield in abundance, there must come the cutting blade of the pruning knife. *'Every branch that bears fruit he prunes, that it may bear more fruit.'* (John 15:2, RAV.)

What does the Master Gardener use for a knife? Suffering and trial were never God's invention or God's intention. But He can use them. In a significant way He can make them instruments of providence.

Disability, disappointment, distress — these prune away human hopes and aspirations. Nevertheless, in a mysterious way, they can do more than we imagine to develop maturity of character.

We shrink from the process. But in God's garden it remains true that 'old growth' can hinder new fruit!

The wisdom of God sometimes allows the blade of adversity to cut into our plans in order that our living shall not be wasted in mere production of leaves and suckers.

Pruning comes in different ways. But behind the blade held by the gardener, is the *blessing* he plans. No gardener prunes for the purpose of hurting the plant.

● **It is the hand of the gardener that plucks.** Sooner or later we have to face the terminal facts of death and bereavement. In Western society these have become taboo subjects. The general public retreats into escapism, and popular theology resorts to sentimentalism. These days nobody dies. They just 'pass on', 'enter into life' or are 'called to higher service'! Death is pictured as a 'friend'.

But the image of death as a friend is *not* a biblical one. *'The last ENEMY that will be destroyed is death.'* (1 Corinthians 15:26, RAV.)

In the face of the ultimate human dilemma, 'WHY' is the crunch question every pastor has to meet. So much suffering is indiscriminate and often unjust. Some promising 'buds' are plucked by death before they have blossomed.

This problem has troubled the mind of man since the dawn of history.

No solution to the problem is valid if it ignores the sovereignty of the gardener.

Faith rests on the word of the only One who ever claimed to have the 'keys of death and the grave'.

A brilliant young student was killed in a road accident. When the news reached his home, the boy's father strode over to the vicarage. He stormed into the parson's study and blurted out, 'Where was your God when my son was killed?' In that difficult moment the vicar simply responded, 'My God was where He was when His own Son was murdered.'

Our problems are so great because our minds are finite and our faith is small.

'She, supposing him to be the gardener, said to him, "Sir, if you have carried him away, tell me where you have laid him. . . ." Jesus said to her, "MARY!"' (John 20:15, 16, RAV.)

At the point of despair and deepest need, God in Christ has a personal word for His children. In many circumstances it would appear true that the hardest thing the Church asks men to believe is that God is love!

Even the cross only makes sense in the light of the empty tomb.

11 CHOSEN WITNESSES

'Him God raised up the third day, and showed him openly; not to all the people, but unto witnesses chosen before of God.' (Acts 10:40.)

At least eleven personal appearances of the risen Lord are recorded in the New Testament. Simon Peter declared that those who saw Him were 'chosen witnesses'. In other words, these 'Easter encounters' were not haphazard, but purposeful.

Examine these events carefully. In the gospel accounts there is a significant pattern. And the sequence reveals the resurrection of Christ as relevant to every aspect of human need.

- *'He appeared to Peter.'* (1 Corinthians 15:5, NIV.)

Those four words are the main clue to a very private Easter interview. After the crucifixion Simon Peter must have been one of the most despondent men in Jerusalem. The 'Big Mouth' had been silenced by shame. Denial had deflated the boasting.

But Jesus was concerned for Peter, even in his despondency.

First, the risen Lord told the women to go and tell His disciples *'and Peter'*. (Mark 16:7.) Then Paul tells of the encounter which confirmed the message of assurance and forgiveness. Later on, in Galilee, there was the threefold commission to replace the threefold denial with a triple command; *' "Feed my lambs," "Tend my sheep," "Feed my sheep." '* (John 21:15-18, RAV.)

Human life can be warped by a sense of failure. To brood over the past so that it stifles confidence, is to spurn the power of the Lord. He can deal with the past, guide the future, and bring release in the here and now!

So the risen Lord comes to straighten out our personal life.

- '*He appeared first to Mary Magdalene.*' (Mark 16:9.)

Those five words announced a glorious episode. Following the crucifixion Mary was probably the most disturbed woman in Jerusalem. The spiritual centre of gravity in her life had been destroyed.

But Jesus was concerned for Mary, even in her distraction.

It was not just an emotional reunion. Jesus showed Mary the reality of His presence to restore in her the capacity to become the first Gospel Evangelist. Jesus lifted Mary out of the pit of personal grief, by giving her a mission of responsibility for others.

'*Do not cling to me, but go to my brethren and tell them. . . .*'

The apostles may well have considered Mary to be potentially unstable. Jesus took the very sensitivity of Mary's temperament and promoted her into the orbit of pastoral ministry!

So the risen Lord comes to straighten out our emotional life.

- '*He appeared to two men walking from Jerusalem into the country.*' (Mark 16:12, LB.)

Here were two people whose outlook on life had been blighted by sudden tragedy. After the crucifixion there were some very disillusioned people in Jerusalem.

But Jesus was concerned for Cleopas and his partner, even in their depression.

They had made the mistake of putting the local news before the Scriptures.

They thought God was dead. In truth He was walking beside them. Remember Jesus deliberately prevented them from recognizing Him. (Luke 24:16.)

You are more likely to deliver truth to someone when he is touching rock bottom than when he is sitting on cloud nine.

Jesus aimed to impart a new dimension to the outlook of

these two men. He took their shortsightedness and focused their minds on the great plan of salvation. ' *"How dull you are!"* ' he answered. ' *"How slow to believe all that the prophets said! Was not the Messiah bound to suffer in this way before entering upon his glory?"* ' (Luke 24:25, 26, REB.)

Still today, millions are depressed by the latest news headlines. Too many Christians are shaken by humanistic philosophies. It's unbelievable what you have to believe to become an unbeliever!

Cleopas was transformed on the Emmaus road because Jesus reversed the order of his thinking. Those who receive Jesus as the 'Living Word' discover that He unlocks the Written Word.

So the risen Lord comes to straighten out our intellectual life.

● *'After eight days Jesus came to Thomas.'* (See John 20:26.)

Thomas has received a bad press. Concentrating on his doubt, we forget what happened on the final journey to Jerusalem. Having been warned of what was coming, the other disciples held back. By contrast, Thomas said, ' *"Let us also go and die with him."* ' (John 11:16, REB.)

But after the crucifixion Thomas must have been one of the most disconsolate men in Jerusalem. Here was an apostle whose devotion to his Master was solid, and whose reasoning was logical. (John 14:5.)

But Jesus was concerned for Thomas, even in his perplexity.

So Thomas doubted when others believed. He had, after all, been absent when the risen Lord had appeared to his fellow disciples. (John 20:24.) But on that special, memorable occasion when Jesus appeared to dispel the doubts of Thomas, He did so with a much deeper reason than merely to satisfy the rather obstinate requirements of the loyal, logical disciple. Immediately after the formal greeting, Jesus addressed himself directly to Thomas: *'Then he said to Thomas, "Reach your finger here; look at my hands. Reach your hand here and put it into my side. Be unbelieving no longer, but believe." '* (John 20:27, REB.) Who had told Jesus the words of Thomas's challenge? Surely, Christ was teaching the whole Upper Room Company that His physical presence was no longer needed to keep Him in communication with His disciples.

The word to Thomas has become recognized by many of the faithful; 'Almighty God, unto whom all hearts are open, all desires known, and from whom no secrets are hidden. . . . '

It was in the light of this revelation that the apostolic company went forward into the openness of fellowship with each other and with the Lord who would remain with them 'until the end of the age'.

So the risen Lord comes to straighten out our devotional life.

- *'He was seen by James.'* (1 Corinthians 15:7, RAV.)

This is the only reference to this special appearance. After the crucifixion James must have been one of the most disconcerted men in Jerusalem. Who was this man? Paul gives a clue in Galatians 1:18, 19 when, reporting a visit to Jerusalem, he records that he saw *'James the Lord's brother'*. James, the son of Zebedee, had been executed some years before this. At the Council of Jerusalem, recorded in Acts 15, James, the Lord's brother, makes his appearance as one of the leaders of the church.

This James had become a leader of the apostolic company, having grown up alongside Jesus in Nazareth. He had been a part of the family friction; one of *'His brothers'* who *'had no faith in him'*. (John 7:5, REB.) It doesn't, of course, say that James hated Jesus. Doubtless when Jesus commenced His ministry and they saw His miracles, His brothers were proud of Him. ' *"You should leave here and go into Judaea,"* ' they told Him, ' *"so that your disciples may see the great things you are doing. No one can hope for recognition if he works in obscurity. If you can really do such things as these, show yourself to the world."* ' (John 7:2-4, REB.)

The problem arose when it came to talk of His Messiahship. The confrontation with the priests and Scribes was both serious and dangerous. Any admiration the brothers had had turned to fear. And fear led to divided loyalties.

But Jesus was concerned for James, even in His dire dilemma.

Are we willing to admit when we're wrong? That some of life's situations are too big for us? Can we be patient and prayerful over family problems and misunderstandings? Jesus came to James to show that even family feuds can be reconciled.

So the risen Lord comes to straighten out our social life.

* *'He was seen by . . . all the apostles.'* (1 Corinthians 15:7.)

After the crucifixion the apostles must have been the most dejected men in Jerusalem. Their desertion of their Master brought them misery and desolation.

But Jesus was concerned for His disciples, even in their dejection.

How did Jesus revive and recommission the apostolic leadership?

He offered inner peace to replace fear: 'Peace be with you.' They knew the Scriptures theoretically, but not experimentally. *'Then he opened their minds to understand the scriptures.'* (Luke 24:45, REB.)

He offered inner purpose to replace frustration: 'So send I you.' Three years before they had been called to become 'fishers of men'. As a team they had been constantly bickering. Now their treasurer had become a traitor and a suicide.

Jesus brought a new commission; *'As the Father has sent me, so send I you.'* In His power 'learners' were to become 'instructors'.

He offered inner power to replace faintheartedness: 'Receive the Holy Spirit.' These men were huddled together for fear of the Jews. Eleven men against the world! Yet, in a generation, their faith had turned the world upside down. *'Jesus breathed on them. . . . '* Humanity began when God breathed into Adam the breath of life. Christianity began when the Second Adam breathed into a new community the heartbeat of redeemed life.

In every age the Church needs to be renewed and revived.

The Church often declares its willingness for Christ to reign over His flock, but Christians are often less anxious to experience His rule.

So the risen Lord comes to straighten out our denominational life.

12 FAILURE? THE WAY BACK

The two disciples *'rose up the same hour, and returned to Jerusalem.'* (Luke 24:33.)

Returning, when it means 'going back', implies retreat. However, sometimes we learn more through a planned withdrawal than an over-hasty leap into No-Man's Land. (Never advance unless your lines of communication with HQ are sure!) Often we discover that happenings that we judge spiritual setbacks can lead to positive progress. What happened to the Emmaus disciples is a dramatic example. After a spiritual defeat they grasped the truth of the risen Lord that enabled them to return to victory.

Three headlines emerge from their experience. When they went back to Jerusalem . . .

● It was a return to a place of failure.

Just three days earlier Jerusalem, for them, had been a scene of denial, defeat and despair. There can be no greater test of character than to go back to a place of defeat — and begin again. Here's a challenge for Christians! After a traumatic event, feelings of bitterness and betrayal can poison our outlook on life. . . .

It is easy to preach that we must forgive and forget. But when it comes to the doing of it . . . Not quite as simple as it sounds.

Forgiveness belongs to God. If someone asks my forgiveness I respond willingly because I remember how Jesus Christ has forgiven me. *Forgetting* is more complicated. There is a sense in which we cannot forget. Seventy years ago an accident almost severed my left thumb. I still bear the scar. But once healed, it has never been a handicap. It is the same in life. A scar is one thing; a festering wound is something quite different. A wounded spirit can become infected by hatred and a desire for revenge.

Two factors in this Emmaus story are a challenge. The return to Jerusalem meant:

No escapism.

Those disciples could have bypassed Jerusalem and trekked north to Galilee. In contemporary terms 'returning to Jerusalem' indicated a willingness to apologize, rather than to seek a new address. Forgiveness needs to be sought by deed as well as by desire;

No excuses.

The return to Jerusalem meant an admission of failure. A fault by any other name is still a defect. Is 'my nerves are bad' a euphemism for 'I have a bad temper'? Can even 'depression' be a cover-up for resentment and jealousy? Or 'absentmindedness' be the result of indiscipline?

On to the next headline.

When the disciples went back to Jerusalem it was:

● A return from a position of faith.

These two disciples believed in the Scriptures. Yet events had shaken their faith and shattered their morale. Two things had been wrong:

Their study had been too narrow: 'He explained to them what was said in all the Scriptures.' (Luke 24:27, NIV.) The trouble was that their vision had been too exclusive. They had dwelt on their favourite passages and built a picture of their own liking. God's people still draw from the Bible the things they want to find there. They put on their blinkers when they encounter passages too hard to take. It is a good thing to desire 'the milk of the word'; but we have to cut our teeth on something more solid. The important thing about your Bible is not whether it has real leather covers, but whether what is between the covers broadens and deepens your understanding of divine truth.

Their hopes had been too selfish: 'We had hoped he would have redeemed Israel.' The trouble was that their reasoning had been too introspective. They had not envisaged that Jesus might redeem the world! Their hope was simple; God was on their side, hell was for the Romans, and they would have the front seats in the kingdom!

Jesus knows and understands the narrowness of man's vision. He made those disciples understand that the love of God is broader than the measure of man's mind. The company of Jesus is a heart-warming experience that guides to maturity of faith.

In relation to the past of those disciples, the return to Jerusalem was a return to a place of failure. In relation to their present, it was a return from a position of faith. In relation to their future, it was

• A return into the power of fellowship.

'They rose up . . . and returned to Jerusalem, and found the eleven gathered together, and them that were with them.' (Luke 24:33.)

Many of life's perplexities are unravelled, not by personal introspection, but through corporate concern. By human design we were born into a family. An abandoned baby is an affront to humanity. By spiritual design we were born again into a Family. A believer without spiritual allegiance is an affront to the divine community. Christian experience is first an encounter with Jesus Christ, but the command of the risen Lord was *'Go tell'* and *'Go into all the world'*.

But those two disciples who left Emmaus for Jerusalem; Who were they about to join?

A company of sinners.

When they reached the upper room they joined a group of fellow-failures. Some people tell me that they will not go to church because there are too many hypocrites there. The simple answer is, There is always room for one more! Christians meet together, not because they are better than others, but because they would be worse apart from God's grace. The miracle is that Christ loves His Church, 'faults and all'. In true worship we extol Christ and encourage one another.

A communion of saints.

In the upper room the group that came together did so, not because of what they had failed to do, but because of all that the Lord had done. When we join the family of God we soon discover that the Heavenly Father has some awkward children. We also begin to realize the miracle of Christ's promise that He will build such a Church that *'the gates of hell shall not prevail against it'*. (Matthew 16:17, 18.)

Therefore, forget the phoneys and the false prophets. . . .

Focus the attention on Jesus and His Word. . . .

Seek to walk in His way and you will never walk alone.

13　THIS IS THE VICTORY

'If Christ has not been raised, then our preaching is in vain and your faith is in vain.' (1 Corinthians 15:14, RSV.)

Paul was on trial for his life. His cross-examiner was a Roman lawyer. King Agrippa presided. The charge arose from his preaching of the resurrection of Jesus.

A phrase grips the mind: *'While he was thus defending himself Festus burst out, "You are raving, Paul! All your learning has driven you mad!" But Paul replied, "I am not mad, your excellency. I speak nothing but the sober truth. The king knows of these matters, and I can speak freely before him. I cannot believe that any of these matters have escaped his notice, for it has been no hole-and-corner business." '* (Acts 26:24-26, JBP.)

Irony of ironies. There are in the Church today theologians who seem to have more in common with Festus than with Paul! Modernist theologians, like agnostics, repeat parrot-fashion that 'it all happened so long ago — no one can be sure'.

Paul was speaking within living memory of the events. The initiative favoured the opposition. All that was required to silence Paul and the preaching of the resurrection was to produce the body of Jesus.

The apostles had lost faith when they knew their Master was dead. They had not expected to see Him again. Now they published far and wide that He was risen from the dead. For forty days He met with them, walked, talked and ate with them.

If there had been the smallest shred of evidence to disprove the resurrection the Jews would have produced it. They failed to do so. *'The Word of God gained more and more ground. The number of disciples in Jerusalem greatly increased, while a considerable proportion of the priesthood accepted the faith.'* (Acts 6:7, JBP.)

The phrase about the priesthood warrants much more attention. Had those Jewish priests been converted solely through apostolic preaching? Carried away on the emotion of the moment?

Very doubtful.

The religious bigot has a closed mind that is rarely changed through argument or debate. Indisputable evidence rather than academic theory brings people to radical change. That 'considerable proportion of the priesthood' had accepted the indisputable evidence, and then taken their acceptance to its logical conclusion.

Some have wondered why the risen Christ did not present Himself before those who were responsible for His execution. Such drama would have produced predictable results. But the kingdom of Jesus Christ does not annex through fear, it attracts through faith. Nevertheless, God does not leave Himself without a witness, and sometimes a 'silent witness' speaks louder than noisy debate.

What was the *'indisputable evidence'* that caused *'a considerable proportion of the priesthood'* to accept *'the Faith'*?

The New Testament mentions *three* Silent Witnesses from those 'Three Days That Shook The World'. Those three silent witnesses challenged 'a considerable proportion of the priesthood' — as well as many of the Jewish people. They challenged them, and they authenticated the claims of the apostles.

The clues that shook the Jews? A curtain, a tombstone and a grave-cloth.

● **The curtain.** *'Behold, the veil of the temple was torn in two from top to bottom.'* (Matthew 27:51, RAV.)

That scrap of information must have come from an 'inside source'. The 'veil of the temple' was of particular significance. The plan of the sanctuary in Jewish tabernacle and temple was identical. There was the Holy Place where priests ministered at Lamp-stand, Table of Shewbread, and Altar of

Incense. There was the Holy of Holies where only the High Priest entered on the Day of Atonement. Between these two compartments was the veil which partitioned the sanctuary. (Hebrews 9:1-7.)

What consternation there must have been behind the scenes in the temple on the afternoon when Jesus died. . . . Some may retort, 'That was in the days of religious superstition and we've outgrown all of that.' I wonder? God can still confront men and women when, in some unexpected way, they find the curtain of the 'inner life' rent asunder. You may replace the curtain, but you cannot erase the revelation.

● **The tombstone.** *'The angel of the Lord . . . came and rolled back the stone . . . and sat upon it.'* (Matthew 28:2.)

The story is fascinating because this fragment of the gospel of Matthew offers a 'key' clue.

Who would imagine that a gravestone could become a vital witness for the defence?

Frank Morison wrote an interesting book entitled *Who Moved the Stone?* The crunch question is not, *'Who* moved the stone?' but *'Why* was it moved, and *where?'* The stone was, apparently, 'very great'. (Mark 16:4.) It would have been a prepared stone to rest in a chiselled-out channel in front of the tomb entrance. 'He rolled a great stone to the door.' (Matthew 27:60.) It needed more than the strength of three women to move it. (Mark 16:3.) A number of these first-century rolling stones can be seen in Jerusalem today. Some weigh more than four tons.

It seems evident that the official guards at the Tomb were a Jewish militia — the men of the temple guard. Pilate told the priests: 'You have a guard.' The 'soldiers' of the Bible record would have consisted of at least four armed men. As the story unfolds we read that the chief priests told their men, ' "If this comes to the governor's ears, we will appease him and make you secure." ' (Matthew 28:14,

RAV.) That clearly implies the guard was not directly under Roman authority. If they had been they would not have reported to the temple authorities.

On that resurrection morning something happened to the stone in front of Joseph's sepulchre that caused the temple policemen to run back to HQ. Matthew's account must have come from an eye-witness — *for only the militia were there!*

Why was the stone moved? One Sunday School answer was: 'To let Jesus out.' We are right to smile at that suggestion. The risen Christ could not be confined by stone or seal. The stone was moved to 'exit the guard'. It may have been moved to make way for 'chosen witnesses' to enter the Tomb. It is clear that the women, at the first light of Sunday morning, had no knowledge of the 'sealing' of the Tomb.

It may seem irrelevant to ask, 'Where was the stone moved?' There are two possible answers. If, like Herod's family tomb which can be seen in Jerusalem today, the sepulchre entrance was below ground level, when the stone is rolled back, one can sit on the 'arch'. A more significant point — from the fourth gospel — is that the stone was 'taken away'. (John 20:1.) For a great stone to be removed from its groove and placed flat on its side would require more than normal manpower!

What a turmoil must have arisen when the Jewish militia arrived back at Temple HQ. Guardsmen in a state of shock. Officials filled with consternation. The chief priests in a rage. Out of the confusion came a strange conclusion: *'Say that his disciples stole the body while you slept.'* (See Matthew 28:11-15.)

The fact that the guard was bribed to give that explanation is staggering! The Jewish leaders must have visited the scene and found it to be impossible to incriminate their men. The facts must have been whispered within temple circles. The silent witness of the great stone must have had an impact upon some within the priesthood.

People's ideas of God can be like that stone. Set. Sealed. Guarded.

Suddenly they have to face some disturbing element of truth that shakes their fixed ideas.

You can't imprison revealed truth.

You may replace the 'stone', but you can never regain the old sense of self-security.

• **A grave-cloth.** *'Simon Peter . . . went into the tomb; and he saw the linen clothes lying there.'* (John 20:6, RAV.)

It was through the Garden Tomb, Jerusalem, that I came to realize the deep, spiritual importance of John chapter 20.

Verse 1: Mary Magdalene (and companions) approach the Tomb and see the stone taken away from the entrance. Without waiting to investigate, Mary runs back with the dramatic but *mistaken* message.

Verse 2: ' *"They have taken away the Lord out of the tomb, and we do not know where they have laid him."* ' This may provide additional evidence as to the position of the stone. If it had been merely rolled to one side, Mary Magdalene would have concluded that others had already entered in.

Verses 3-7: Peter and the Beloved Disciple run to the Tomb. The younger man arrives first and stoops to look in but does not enter. Why not? In the light of Mary's statement he was expecting to find the Tomb empty. Yet as he looks into the semi-darkness he can see the outline of a body lying in the sepulchre. He is too bewildered to move. 'Poor Mary,' he thinks, 'she has become mentally confused.' Simon Peter arrives — and rushes in. *'He saw the linen clothes lying there, and the handkerchief that had been around his head, not lying with the linen clothes, but folded together in a place by itself.'* In other words, the grave-clothes were unruffled and undisturbed, and Jesus was not there.

Verse 8: *'Then the other disciple, who came to the tomb first, went in also; and he saw and believed.'* Peter sees that, although there is the appearance of a body in the tomb, the grave-clothes are empty. He recognizes that no human hand could remove a corpse from linen winding-bands without leaving signs of disarrangement.

Verse 10: *'Then the disciples went away again to their own home.'* There is no use searching for a body. Their eyes have seen a wonder greater than human minds can fathom. *'These are written that you may believe.'* (John 20:31, RAV.)

The question arises, 'How can these verses from the New Testament relate to the Jewish leaders?'

There can be no doubt that some chief priests must have entered the Tomb when they inspected the situation. Some must have seen the 'silent witness' grave-clothes just as the disciples had seen them. They too could not fail to grasp the significance.

People are guilty of treating the Gospel as a dead thing.

In one sense, the Jesus of history has no more claim on us than a corpse. We can honour His memory and sing hymns in tribute to the beauty of His life.

Suddenly we are confronted with a new dimension. We are confronted with that dimension where we see the evidence of His power at work in human lives today.

Men think that they can lock Him out. But He has a master key.

'Behold, I am alive for ever more, and have the keys of death and the grave.' (See Revelation 1:18.)

I wonder what happened to those 'empty grave-clothes'?

Weeks later the Jewish leaders heard the apostles preaching in the centre of Jerusalem — just a few minutes' walk from the Garden and the Tomb of Joseph of Arimathea. They sought to refute the message, but they could not erase from their memories the Curtain . . . the Tombstone . . . and the grave-clothes.

To face up to the evidence for the resurrection of Jesus Christ means facing up to the ultimate.

'*We are citizens of Heaven; our outlook goes beyond this world to the hopeful expectation of the Saviour who will come from Heaven, the Lord Jesus Christ. He will remake these wretched bodies of ours to resemble his own glorious body, by that power of his which makes him the master of everything that is.*' (Philippians 3:20, 21, JBP.)

14 THE BELOVED DISCIPLE

New Testament scholars suggest that Simon Peter was a guiding hand behind the authorship of Mark's gospel. Hence it has a short, sharp, clipped, headlong quality of a first-person account. But the more reflective fourth gospel was also, remember, a firsthand account. . . .

When we read John's gospel carefully we discern that parts of the text reveal, in a shy sort of way, information and details that do not appear in the other three gospels. There are incidents that clearly involved the writer and the Lord. When relating some of these incidents John 'veils' his identity with the phrase 'the disciple whom Jesus loved'.

To get as much as possible out of the firsthand insights let us spotlight these 'beloved disciple' passages. There are five of them towards the end of John's gospel.

● *'Now the disciple whom Jesus loved was leaning on Jesus' shoulder.'* (See John 13:23.)

The scene: the upper room. The time: the night of His betrayal.

There is consternation among the apostles at the suggestion of a traitor in their midst. Simon Peter signals the Beloved Disciple to ask Jesus to identify the betrayer. *'Lord, who is it?'* he whispers. *'It is he to whom I shall give the sop.'*

It is vital to understand that at communal meals in New Testament times, diners were not seated on chairs, but reclined on rugs and cushions. The fact that Judas was reclining next to the Master, on His other side, makes it clear that Christ's words were whispered into the ear of the Beloved Disciple. This explains why the remainder of the company did not hear what was said.

The Beloved Disciple, it will be remembered, was *leaning*. In such an atmosphere leaning upon the Lord becomes the secret of serenity.

● *'Jesus saw his mother, and the disciple whom he loved standing by . . . . '* (John 19:26, RAV.) What a different scene faces us here. To that disciple it must have seemed that a whole lifetime had passed since the meal in the Upper Room. But it was less than twenty hours! Life's major crises often come with paralysing suddenness. A phone call? A policeman at the door? It is not a morbid thing to anticipate reaction to tragedy, grief and pain. Is our faith geared to meet a crisis?

Back at the Calvary scene. Where was Simon Peter? Where were the others who had pledged such loyalty to Jesus? Is it a coincidence that the only disciple found standing at the cross is the one who *leaned* on Jesus at the Last Supper?

Now it was the Lord who needed someone to meet *His* request. *'Son, behold your mother.'* The one who had *leaned* is the one now *standing* ready for service. Those who *lean* on Jesus through their life of faith, are those most likely to *stand* for Jesus in the fight of faith.

● *'Mary came to Simon Peter and the other disciple whom Jesus loved. They both ran . . . that other disciple outran Peter. . . . '* (See John 20:1-4.)

Sunday morning, first light. There have been hours of misery and despair. Yet, the one who first leaned and then stood is now seen *running*.

The first thing to learn from this incident? Never take rumour as 'Gospel'. Mary was confused as she approached the Tomb. *'They have taken the Lord out of the sepulchre. . . .'* She jumped to a false conclusion, and gave a wrong message. The Beloved Disciple did not become paralysed by new despair. In *running* to the scene of reported disaster he discovers evidence of history's greatest triumph.

Do we ever misinterpret the events that form the pattern of our daily life? If we allow our minds to focus on a single aspect of social history or contemporary events, we may become convinced that the devil is in control of our universe. The sceptic cries, 'If there is a God, why doesn't He *do* something?' The prophet declares, *'They that wait upon the Lord shall renew their strength; . . . they shall run, and not be weary.'* (Isaiah 40:31.) The Beloved Disciple who was first *leaning*, and then *standing* was still *running* when all seemed lost!

● *'When Jesus stood on the shore the disciple whom Jesus loved said, It is the Lord.'* (See John 21:4-7.)

Weeks had passed. The disciples had felt restless. 'I'm going fishing,' Peter had said. 'Me too,' others had echoed. 'That night they caught nothing,' reports John. After some vital spiritual experience, how easy it is to drift back to the old routine. Nothing wrong with fishing. It just indicates that their outlook was still anchored in the past.

One man was alert for a new vision. The disciple whom Jesus loved was *looking*. Vision is the dynamic of progressive discipleship. The Beloved Disciple was quick to discern the Lord's presence. This had been the progression: LEANING-STANDING-RUNNING-LOOKING.

● *'Peter saw the disciple whom Jesus loved following and said, What shall this man do?'* (See John 21:20, 21.)

The scene: still the shoreline of Galilee. Jesus and His disciples were walking. Peter began to ply Jesus with questions. He was curious about the destiny of the others and, as Jesus knew, such curiosity often leads to unwarranted speculation about the future. How many hours, days and nights do people spend worrying about the future? Here, however, Peter was not only preoccupied with the future; he was meddling in other people's concerns.

The Beloved Disciple was *following*, according to the text, when Peter asked his question. No doubts or fears, just a great confidence born of faith in Christ.

When he came to pen the fourth gospel years later most

of the other soldiers of the cross had fallen at their posts. He did not know whether he would tarry until the Lord's return. It didn't much matter. He was content to be found:

LEANING - STANDING - RUNNING - LOOKING - FOLLOWING.

15 SECRET SESSION

'He showed himself alive after his passion by many infallible proofs, being seen of them forty days.' (Acts 1:3.)

If the resurrection message seems to be losing relevance to modern churchmen, perhaps it is because theological minds have grown dull to the magnitude of the truth Christians possess.

The revival of ancient heresies in the garb of so-called New Age theories have so blurred the vision of some that the very ground of our faith is turned into a platform of psychic illusion.

By contrast the New Testament insists that the resurrection of the Lord Jesus Christ was *not* a subjective experience by a few people that, in the telling, was amplified by mass hysteria. A spirit does *not* eat *'broiled fish and honeycomb'*. (Luke 24:42, 43.) A vision does *not* kindle a fire on the beach and cook breakfast. (John 21:9, 12.) Yet facts like these were at the heart of apostolic preaching. *'God raised him to life on the third day, and allowed him to be clearly seen.'* (Acts 10:40, REB.) If you want to propound a theology that excludes the physical resurrection of Jesus you will not be talking about the faith of the gospels.

The Resurrection was not a figment of excited imagination; it was Jesus who had conquered death and who, in a unique and glorified body came to give men assurance of immortality through His resurrection.

'He was seen by them for forty days.' Why do we not hear more about that? There was no shortage of material. Indeed, John wrote, *'If it were all to be recorded in detail, I suppose the world could not hold the books that would be written.'* (John 21:25, REB.) That we appear to know less than we would wish may be significant. The early church was *making* history, not *writing* it. Their mission was not to document the past, but to dynamite the present. The apostles did not

publicize a redundant cemetery. They preached a risen Christ. These 'followers of the Way' were not interested in the place where Christ's body had lain. Their priority was to prepare for the promise that, in a global sense, He was going to reign.

Gospel history was not a symposium from memory's lumber room. It was a serial story that would be written in the sweat and blood of persecution. Something had happened that changed those timid disciples into men of conviction and courage. It is wise to retrace steps in the Gospel records to make sure we do not overlook important facts from the great forty-day period.

Two verses may have particular importance:

'The eleven disciples made their way to Galilee, to the mountain where Jesus had told them to meet him.' (Matthew 28:16, REB.)

'Then he appeared to over five hundred of our brothers at once, most of whom are still alive, though some have died.' (1 Corinthians 15:6, REB.)

In isolation, the last reference is a puzzling verse. It is likely that, when Paul wrote those words, he was referring to the same event recorded in Matthew 28:16. In other words, when the risen Lord appeared on the mountain of Galilee, it was to the apostolic circle plus a great company of over 500 believers! Unless we link these two verses, the isolation of the 'eleven disciples' is illogical.

• Why send the Eleven to Galilee? Their HQ was in Jerusalem, the obvious geographical focus for outreach.

• Why send the Eleven to a mountain? The Upper Room had become a place of meeting.

• Why fix an appointment? Jesus could come to them at any time. They expected His appearance.

All these facts make the event pointless if it relates to just eleven people. But, supposing Jesus wanted a 'secret session' with all who had loved and followed Him during the days of His ministry. Jerusalem had been the 'launching pad', but Galilee had been the 'seed bed'. The ministry that *ended* in Jerusalem, *began* in Galilee. More than half of the three-year ministry of Jesus had taken place there. Is it likely that He would forget the contacts who had brought Him joy? From the first He gathered round Him a little army of devoted followers; now they were to be mobilized for a campaign beyond their wildest dreams.

This mountain reunion must have been carefully planned.

Remember how Simon Peter and the others returned to their old haunts, grew restless and went fishing. They caught nothing. Jesus taught them a lesson and called them to breakfast. (John 21.) This may well have been the moment when the details of the 'secret session' were disclosed. The date and place of the meeting, the names of those to be invited, the time of assembly. Plans would have been announced, and the apostles would have been briefed for the operation.

Then came the day! From all the districts round the Lake, little groups began to leave the villages. Could it have taken place on the Sabbath? And at a favourite spot in the hills recalling the Sermon on the Mount?

The apostles would have been early, as all good stewards should be. The assembly would gather together. What an atmosphere. There would be a buzz of incredulous chatter until, as the appointed time drew near, there would be a hush of expectancy. . . .

Then . . . *He came.* No sudden appearance. He, who refused the tempter's invitation to be spectacular, would not use His power to startle His friends. Perhaps a shepherd's song heralded His approach. Then, round a curve of the hill, He moved towards them. '*When they saw him, they knelt in worship, though some were doubtful.*' (Matthew 28:17, REB.) Those last four words assure me of the veracity of the Gospel. No propagandist would ever include a hint of doubt in the story. The phrase would never refer to the apostles, but to some at the very back of the throng who may have experienced a moment of incredulity. Firm faith is sometimes a gradual and growing experience.

Soon the Saviour was in the midst of them as they crowded round Him in inexpressible ecstasy. It is not necessary to rely too much on imagination to guess some of those who would have been there. Apart from the apostolic contingent, we conjecture that Jairus would be present, together with a daughter now aged 15. (Jesus always has time for teen-agers!) The couple from Cana may have brought children for a blessing. The men from Gadara had made it.

Jesus lives to rid mankind of morbid fear and deadly delusion. So, we could go right down the line of that happy 500. For each and every one there was a personal word and benediction.

Can all this be relevant to our twentieth-century situation? Jesus said, *'Because I live, you shall live also.'* The 'secret session' in Galilee becomes a time capsule and a new reality. The atmosphere of spiritual victory is still present in every assembly where Jesus Christ is received and honoured. When the Church bows to His authority it renews its vitality.

One reaction to the mountain meeting in Galilee may be to wonder what Jesus said to the 500. We *do* know something! *'Jesus came near and said to them: "Full authority in heaven and on earth has been committed to me. Go therefore to all nations and make them my disciples; baptize them in the name of the Father and the Son and the Holy Spirit, and teach them to observe all things that I have commanded you. I will be with you always, to the end of time."'* (Matthew 28:18-20, REB.)

The Authorized Version translation, *'All power is given unto me'*, is familiar to most Christians. It is a heart-lifting assertion. A phrase that rings and echoes down the arches of the ages to our own day. There was no ecclesiastical ex-clusivism about that phrase. The great commission was to *all*. Down the arches of the ages we hear the echo of those words and know that the commission is to *us*.

We live in a world that is spiritually parched and dry. Under a sophisticated exterior society is thirsting for the water of life. Surely that places a special responsibility on Christians.

In the Middle East there is an ancient proverb: 'The sin of the desert is to know where the water is, and not to tell. . . .'

16 ASCENSION

'As they were looking on, he was lifted up, and a cloud took him out of their sight.' (Acts 1:9, RSV.)

The ascension of Jesus has become a neglected part of the gospel narrative.

Ascension is an embarrassment to modern minds.

Academics claim intellectual difficulties about the story and suggest we must see it as 'symbolic rather than historic'.

We need have no such 'hang-up'. If we accept the physical resurrection of Jesus Christ, the objections to His ascension have no substance. Belief in the physical resurrection of Jesus *necessitates* belief in an ascension.

Jesus was not some prototype astronaut. He is Lord of creation who, by His victory over death, had lifted manhood above the gravity of sin's attraction, provided the means of man's salvation, and prepared him for the atmosphere of heaven's communion.

The ascension was a 'teaching aid' in dramatic form. It was the Lord's thoughtful conclusion to the training of the forty days. The apostles had to be shown that a new chapter was about to begin. There must be no doubt or confusion.

Luke records that after the ascension event 'they . . . returned to Jerusalem with great joy'. (Luke 24:52.) What a remarkable phrase! We associate farewells with sorrow. Jesus had so 'weaned' His disciples to become independent of His physical presence, that the ascension brought them joy and not the 'jitters'!

During the weeks of training Jesus had established three factors which should lift our thinking above the narrow dimension of our mortality:

● **Jesus had broken the sound barrier.**

The apostles had grasped that contact with Jesus was no longer dependent on that which is tangible and audible. That much had been made clear to Thomas. Every believer could now establish direct communication with the Lord; *'For through him we both have access in one Spirit to the Father.'* (Ephesians 2:18, RSV.)

- **Jesus had broken the space barrier.**

The apostles had grasped that Jesus was no longer confined by material or geographical boundaries. If the walls of the Tomb and the Upper Room could not impede Him, neither could any other obstruction. The apostles had not ceased to worship in the temple, but they knew that from then on no Jew, Roman or Greek could ever confine the presence of Jesus to a religious sanctuary.

- **Jesus had broken the time barrier.**

The apostles had learned that to trust Christ's command for the time to come was the safest way to see God's will done. From the ascension angels the apostles had learned that *'This same Jesus, which is taken up from you into heaven, shall so come in like manner as ye have seen him go into heaven.'* (Acts 1:11.) But, from Jesus Himself, seconds before, they had heard *'It is not for you to know the times or the seasons, which the Father hath put in his own power.'* (Acts 1:7.) Long-term guidance is best found through short-term obedience. And they had the emphatic promise of the Saviour; *'I will be with you always, to the end of time.'* (Matthew 28:20, REB.)

What is the present relevance of the ascension for Christians?

- **It doesn't matter where you live.**

Climate, custom and circumstance may dictate the location of our habitation, but need not isolate us from the Lord. Jesus Christ is a Universal Saviour. A Scottish lady once asked me for an address in Israel; 'My daughter is ill and if I can take her to the Holy Land she will be healed.' Firmly, but gently,

I had to say, 'If you cannot prove the Power of Jesus in Glasgow, you will not find it in Galilee.' God's salvation can never be confined by the boundaries of race, nationality or creed, and His grace cannot be limited by denominational barriers.

● It doesn't matter when you live.

History has much to teach us. Nevertheless, whether a person is born in the first or the twenty-first century does not affect God's plan of salvation. Millions become muddled because down the centuries the Church has allowed basic Bible teaching to be infiltrated by doctrines that mix up time and eternity. At the judgement seat of Christ, Simon Peter and the apostles will stand on precisely the same ground as all other Christians. If we are wise we shall leave eternal issues with God.

These days liberal preachers say, 'We must adapt our ethics to relate to the situation of our age.' Have nothing to do with such ideas. *'Your word is everlasting, Lord; it is firmly fixed in heaven.'* (Psalm 119:89, REB.)

Our intellect is limited, finite. God is unlimited, infinite. There are many baffling issues that we shall only grasp when God reveals them to us in His own good time. *'Eye has not seen, nor ear heard, nor have entered into the heart of man the things which God has prepared for those who love him.'* (1 Corinthians 2:9, RAV.)

● It doesn't matter how long you live.

Life is a precious gift to be lived to the full. Life is for living! But the New Testament is utterly opposed to the notion that death is the worst thing that can happen to us. Jesus taught, *'Fear not those who can kill the body. . . .'* Paul wrote, *'Whether we live, we live unto the Lord; and whether we die, we die unto the Lord: whether we live therefore, or die, we are the Lord's.'* (Romans 14:8.)

In our materialist society the Christian view of mortality

is often overlaid with an unscriptural attitude to death. The quality of life is more important than length of days.

From the Mount of the Ascension the apostles headed back to the Upper Room. Echoing in their minds were the parting words of the angels; ' *"Men of Galilee . . . this same Jesus, who was taken up from you . . . will so come in like manner as you saw him go."* ' (Acts 1:10, 11, RAV.)

It is the Blessed Hope of the ages!

Because of that hope, we may hold our heads high in the air — *if our feet are firmly on the ground.* During a Holy Land pilgrimage one minister remarked, 'I saw teardrops of emotion as people sang, "I walked today where Jesus walked".' He added, 'One day, I'll hope to see beads of perspiration as they say, "I've served today as Jesus served".'

17 PENTECOST — THEN AND NOW

'The day of Pentecost had come, and they were all together in one place. . . . They were all filled with the Holy Spirit. . . . ' (Acts 2:1, 4, REB.)

'Pentecost' comes from the Greek for fifty. It was observed on the fiftieth day after Passover (Deuteronomy 16:9).

It was a joyful feast that marked the birth of the Christian Church.

What was the outcome of events on that special Pentecost day?

'The multitude of them that believed were of one heart and one soul. . . . And with great power gave the apostles witness of the resurrection of the Lord Jesus: and great grace was upon them all.' (Acts 4:32, 33.)

New truth in the temple. No sooner had the Spirit's fire descended than the multi-lingual multitude in Jerusalem for the feast, perhaps influenced by the *'strong, driving wind'* (Acts 2:2, REB), surged in the direction of the centre of festivity. It would appear that the apostles themselves made their way from 'the house where they were sitting' (Acts 2:2) in the direction of the temple (Acts 2:4-6). Doubtless this was where the multitude would converge when they perceived that an inexplicable event was taking place. Hence the temple was almost certainly the setting for Peter's Pentecost sermon.

A poignant scene, this. Peter stood in the place where Jesus had been rejected and announced that 'God had spoken' and Jesus had been raised from the dead!

A new community in an old city. The Spirit did not immediately disperse the apostles to 'foreign fields'. Instead, He transformed their ministry in the local situation.

The new community — which continued to worship in

the temple (Luke 24:53) — did not preach a social Gospel. But they did take care of the poor among them. (Acts 2:44-47.) Peter's Pentecost sermon was a powerful appeal for the Jews to accept their Messiah. It was replete with allusions to Old Testament prophecy. This at once authenticated Jesus as Messiah *and* provided legitimacy for the preaching of the 'followers of the Way'. It concluded with a powerful appeal; *'Repent, and be baptized every one of you in the name of Jesus Christ for the remission of sins, and ye shall receive the gift of the Holy Ghost. For the promise is unto* **you***, and to* **your children***, and to* **all that are afar off, even as many as the Lord our God shall call***.'* (Acts 2:38, 39, italics supplied.)

An offer of missionary service in lands beyond the seas can often seem more attractive than a call to labour in an urban parish back home. Before we accept a candidate for the Foreign Field we ought to examine what he has done on the Home Front. He may speak the language of Zion, but has he also helped to 'build the walls of Jerusalem'? The spiritual revival that was Pentecost was typified by wind and fire. Too often modern revivalism is characterized by 'hot air' and 'sparks'.

A new dynamic in the same disciples. New Testament 'pentecostalism' was not evidenced by loss of self-control, but by very significant God-control. The crucial fact about Pentecost was *not* 'tongues'; though the fact that a multi-lingual 'congregation' heard *'every man in his own tongue wherein he was born'* (see Acts 2:8) is certainly astounding. The really significant thing, however, was that the apostles proclaimed Jesus Christ as Messiah of Israel and Universal Saviour and Sovereign.

The second great thing about Pentecost is that *the very same disciples*, who had fled from Gethsemane and, in the main, been conspicuous by their absence when Jesus was on trial and on Calvary, now preached the Gospel of the empty cross and the empty tomb without the slightest hint of reserve. Indeed they preached their Gospel 'with power'?

Because of Christ's resurrection and ascension, the life of the Holy Spirit is available to all who will receive. This was the fulfilment of the prophecy made by Jesus in the Jerusalem temple at the height of the concluding Sabbath of the Feast of Tabernacles; ' *"Whoever believes in me, as scripture says, 'Streams of living water shall flow from within him."* ' (John 7:37, 38, REB.) In case readers of his gospel should miss the point, John went on to explain, *'He was speaking of the Spirit which believers in him would later receive; for the Spirit had not yet been given, because Jesus had not yet been glorified.'* (Verse 39, REB.)

Calvary proclaims pardon. Pentecost proclaims power.

Many Christians appear to be stationed on the right side of Calvary but on the wrong side of Pentecost. Experientially the two events are linked. If we have not received redemption at the cross, we cannot carry the torch of Pentecostal fire.

A pastor was called to minister in a very run-down parish. Church officials warned him, 'You will gain no response from this congregation.' The next week a large notice was posted outside the building: THIS CHURCH IS DEAD. The Funeral Service will take place on Wednesday next at 3pm.

Out of curiosity a large number attended. A coffin had been placed in the chancel and, as a 'last rite', those present were invited to file past. It was an open coffin and, as each looked inside, there was simply a large mirror that reflected the personal features of each mourner. . . .

How willing is God to give the gift of His Spirit and the regeneration that comes with it? Listen to Jesus; *'If you then, who are evil, know how to give good gifts to your children, how much more will the Heavenly Father give the Holy Spirit to those who ask him!'* (Luke 11:13, RSV.)

When Paul went to Ephesus he put a question to a small group of religious activists: ' *"Did you receive the Holy Spirit when you became believers?"* ' (Acts 19:2, REB.) This group must have been steeped in the observances of Judaism. For all that, they were conscious that their religion had an end in view, and a future in store. Their minds had been opened to John the Baptist who had announced the coming of Messiah. But, so far, they had failed to see that Jesus was the Christ foretold in all the Scriptures.

The point of that Pauline incident is this: The key to the Holy Spirit's indwelling is related to a revelation of the Person of the Lord Jesus Christ. Paul asked his 'leading question' because he had detected a deficiency in the group. Directly they were enlightened by the Gospel of the death and resurrection of Jesus, everything was changed in their life and experience. In this new dimension of spiritual truth was the ignition for spiritual revival. The gift of the Holy Spirit that accompanied faith in Christ then drove a dynamic and developing Church.

Eight years later Paul wrote one of the most inspiring of his church letters. Little wonder that, in this Ephesian letter, there are so many references to the influence of the Holy Spirit. Let's look at the 'hallmarks' of the Spirit Paul revealed in this letter to the young Church in Ephesus:

● **The Spirit seals.** *'Having believed, you were sealed with the Holy Spirit of promise.'* (Ephesians 1:13, RAV.) This 'seal' was a mark of possession; possession by God. When we have realized the purchase price of our redemption, the Holy Spirit brings to our understanding the spiritual status that God places on every true believer.

● **The Spirit guarantees.** *'The Holy Spirit is the earnest of our inheritance.'* The Holy Spirit is the *earnest of our redemption.* An 'earnest' was a regular feature of Greek business life; the price of anything paid in advance as a guarantee that the rest would, in due time, be paid. Paul is saying that the experience of the Holy Spirit which we have in this world is a foretaste of the blessedness of heaven; and it is the guarantee that some day we will enter into full possession of the blessedness of God.

● **The Spirit unifies.** *'Walk worthy of your calling . . . endeavouring to keep the unity of the Spirit.'* (See Ephesians 4:1-3.) 'Unity' has been a theological 'in-word' for about eighty years now. Communities have arisen to pray and work for unity. That is good, but not entirely 'focal'. The New Testament injunction is that we should keep (or maintain) something that is already operative. Where Christ is Lord, unity is assured. So much debate is expended in attempts to effect a uniformity that savours more of regimentation than dedication. We are 'exhorted' to 'earnestly contend for the faith' (Jude 3) because men so often corrupt it. We must endeavour to grasp the unity of the faith because the Spirit creates it. World councils may settle for a lowest common denominator as a basis for Church union; but Holy Scripture signifies the highest common factor of Christ's redemption as the banner of universal acclamation. (Revelation 7:9, 10.)

The vital tenets of Christian faith are non-negotiable.

In our New Testament, the Holy Spirit is symbolized in terms of wind and fire. Wind and fire can be disturbing elements. In a Spirit-filled church there are likely to be uncomfortable pews. The fire that warms and comforts can also reduce to ashes. But there are certain things that fire can purify but not destroy. (1 Corinthians 3:11-13.) Whatever is of Christ in our lives will endure.

Wind, also, can be an agent of change, sweeping away all that is insecure and unstable.

G. K. Chesterton described the apostolic Church as 'a winged thunderbolt of everlasting enthusiasm'. Their message: The Lord crucified and risen; salvation and righteousness to be found only in Him. The centre of their worship: the Lord's table. Their mission: that every knee shall bow and every tongue confess that 'Jesus is Lord'. Their hope: Maranatha — Lord, come! (1 Corinthians 16:22.)

The Spirit was the winged thunderbolt. When Jesus *ascended* to the throne at His Father's right hand, the Spirit *descended* to His throne. And the throne of the Spirit is the blessed company of all believers.

Psalm 133, NIV, challenges that believing company; 'How good and pleasant it is when brothers live together in unity! It is like precious oil. . . . ' This refers to the anointing of Aaron as High Priest in Israel. Oil is a biblical symbol of the Spirit's activity, and in 1 Peter 2:9 there is implication that Aaron's consecration is a pattern for Christian discipleship.

'It is like precious oil upon the head. . . . ' — *MIND.*

If we wish to enjoy spiritual unity we must be ready for the Holy Spirit to affect our thinking. Remember, the Pentecostal gift was characterized by fire in the upper room — not fog in the upper storey! Over the centuries pride and prejudice have too often constricted the minds of Christians.

'Oil . . . running down on the beard. . . . ' — *MOUTH.*

Truths that touch human hearts find expression in speech and song. The young Church knew this. . . . *'Through Jesus, therefore, let us continually offer to God a sacrifice of praise — the fruit of lips that confess his name.'* (Hebrews 13:15, NIV.) The consecration of emotional capacity is demonstrated through a spirit of praise.

'Oil . . . ran down . . . onto the border of his robe . . . ' — *MOVEMENT.*

Aaron was consecrated from 'top to toe'! In symbol we see that the anointing which the Psalmist describes, relates not only to heart and mind but to motivated activity . . . *'As you have . . . received Christ Jesus the Lord, so walk in him.'* (Colossians 2:6, RAV.) Notice further how the Psalm links the two metaphors. The unity of believers is like oil (verse 2) and like dew (verse 3). Oil is the anointing of

the Spirit; an endowment (once for all). Dew is an appropri-
ation of the Spirit; a process (day by day).

This comparison of the Spirit's gifts with dew suggests
that blessings of spiritual refreshment needs to be received
'new every morning'. I have seen in Jerusalem how the dew
is a silent miracle of natural renewal. Paul wrote: *'This is
the will of God, even your sanctification.'* (1 Thessalonians
4:3.) This links both symbols of oil and dew. Sanctification
is both an act of God and a development of our character.

May the Spirit's anointing affect our thinking, speaking
and living.

May the Spirit's enabling refresh us body, soul and spirit,
now and always.